Charles Barton, James Philemon Holcombe, Francis Bacon

History of a suit in equity

Charles Barton, James Philemon Holcombe, Francis Bacon
History of a suit in equity
ISBN/EAN: 9783743377233

Manufactured in Europe, USA, Canada, Australia, Japa

Cover: Foto ©ninafisch / pixelio.de

Manufactured and distributed by brebook publishing software (www.brebook.com)

Charles Barton, James Philemon Holcombe, Francis Bacon

History of a suit in equity

Barton's History

OF A

SUIT IN EQUITY.

HISTORY

OF A

SUIT IN EQUITY

FROM ITS

Commencement to its Final Termination,

By CHARLES BARTON,
OF MIDDLE TEMPLE.

NEW EDITION, REVISED AND ENLARGED

WITH

FORMS OF BILLS, ANSWERS, PLEAS, DEMURRERS, AND DECREES.

By JAMES P. HOLCOMBE.

AND

AN APPENDIX,

Containing the Rules of Practice for the Courts of Equity of the United States, revised to date, the Statute Laws of the United States relating to Equity, and the Ordinances of Lord Bacon.

CINCINNATI:
ROBERT CLARKE & CO.
1877.

Entered according to Act of Congress, in the year 1847,

BY DERBY, BRADLEY & CO.

In the Clerk's Office of the District Court, for the District of Ohio.

Entered according to Act of Congress, in the year 1877,

BY ROBERT CLARKE & CO.

In the Office of the Librarian of Congress at Washington.

Stereotyped by OGDEN, CAMPBELL & CO., Cincinnati.

PREFACE.

IN reproducing the "HISTORY OF A SUIT IN EQUITY," the editor has taken several liberties with the original work. All the matter relating to the Court of Exchequer (which is now useless, even in England, the Equity jurisdiction of that Court having been taken away by statute), and many explanations of minute points of practice, which have never prevailed in any portion of this country, have been omitted. The notes of Mr. Barton have, for the most part, been incorporated with the text, and the latter has been enlarged by the addition of a variety of new matter, particularly on the subject of Bills, Demurrers, Pleas, Answers and Decrees. Numerous forms of pleadings have been inserted in their appropriate place, borrowed principally from the best English and American treatises. It is proper to mention among the former the works of Smith, Willis, Seaton, and Van Heythusen, and among the latter those of Barbour, Hoffman, Blake, and Edwards. The volume, as it is now presented to the junior members of the profession, will form, it is believed, a more modern and complete outline both of Pleading and Practice in Equity.

To increase the practical value of this volume, we append to it the Rules of Practice for the Courts of Equity of the United States, the Statute Laws of the United States relating to Equity, now in force, and also, on account of their great historical interest, the celebrated Ordinances of Lord Chancellor Bacon.

The student will find it profitable to compare the practice of the Court as now settled with the outline that in the beginning of the seventeenth century was chalked out by the genius of Lord Bacon. On rising from the study of these celebrated Ordinances, he will be able to appreciate the justice of the following beautiful eulogy upon their merit, which was pronounced by the late Justice Story before the Suffolk Bar:—" Under the guidance of Lord Bacon, the business of Chancery assumed a regular course; and at the distance of two centuries, his Ordinances continue to be the pole-star which directs the practice of that Court. A more noble homage to his memory, or a more striking proof of the wisdom and comprehensiveness of his views, can scarcely be imagined. And it may be truly affirmed that his *Novum Organum* scarcely introduced a more salutary change in the study of physics and experimental philosophy, than did his Ordinances in the practical administration of Equity."

FEBRUARY, 1877.

ANALYTICAL TABLE.

INTRODUCTION.

Of the rise and progress of the equitable jurisdiction of the Court of Chancery, ...	25
This court imagined to have arisen from the Wittenagemote of the Saxon Government, . .	25
The Wittenagemote gave rise to the *Aula Regis*,	26
A similar court in other European nations, . [*note*]	26
The monarch at first presided in the *Aula Regis* in person, and was succeeded by the *Grand Justicier*,	26
At the accession of William I, the *Aula Regis* became King's Court Baron, ...	27
This was a principal cause of the Chancellor's equitable jurisdiction, ...	27
This officer was the King's secretary, and the *registrar* of the decrees of the *Aula Regis*, . . .	27
His authority was at first *occasional*, but afterward became *permanent*, ...	27
This officer, among the feudal nations, as the King's secretary, granted the charters for fiefs, which was a source of much power, . . . [*note*]	27

His authority, however, was only *appellate*, and not *original*, until Edward I, ... 28

His *original* jurisdiction much extended by an act in that King's reign, giving him power to frame *new writs*, ... 28

Bishop Waltham was not the inventor of the writ of subpena, ... 30

Ineffectual attempts of the Commons to curb the growing power of Chancery, ... 29

The decisions of the court were for a long time desultory and uncertain, ... 30

Its practice much improved by Lord Bacon, . . 31

Character of Sir Heneage Finch, . . . 31

Eloquent and accurate account of the origin of equitable jurisdiction, by Sir James Macintosh, ... [*note*] 31, 32, 33

Chancery interposed in early times, not from any defect in the common law, but to protect the weak from the strong, ... [*note*] 33

Difficulty of accurately describing the jurisdiction of Chancery, ... 33

A copious source of its present authority is to supply the defects of the common law, . . . 35

An enumeration, by Lord Redesdale, of the various grounds for the interposition of a Court of Chancery, ... [*note*] 35

Chancery compels a discovery of facts by the oath of the defendant, ... 36

Matters of *account, fraud, accident, mistake*, and *trust*, are more particularly cognizable in equity, . . 37

Courts of Equity are considered *extraordinary* tribunals, and only to be resorted to where the *ordinary* tribunals give no relief, ... 38

In England, at this time, the Chancellor is assisted by a Master of the Rolls and three Vice-Chancellors, ... [*note*] 38

The Chancellor, since 1831, relieved from matters in bankruptcy, except on appeal, . . [*note*] 39

The Federal Courts of the United States have equitable jurisdiction and closely conform to the English system, ... [*note*] 39

In most of the States the same tribunal has a common law side and a chancery side, . [*note*] 39

CHAPTER I.

OF INSTITUTING A SUIT IN EQUITY.

A suit is commenced on the part of an individual by a *bill;* on behalf of government, by an *information,* 40

The simple form of an ancient bill given in note, . 40

General description of ancient bills, . [*note*] 40, 41

Any person not laboring under special disability, such as infancy, coverture, or lunacy, may sue in equity, ... 42

Husband should join with wife, unless she claims adversely to him; but if so, she may sue by *next friend,* 42

Next friend may sue for infant, but is responsible for costs, ... 42

Lunatic sues by his committee, ... 42

Bills are *original,* or not original, ... 42

Original bills, which bring any matter before the court for the first time, may *ask relief,* or may not, 42

The recent rules in England, and in the Supreme
Court of the United States, have exemplified the
form and structure of bills, ... 43

Convenient, in analysis, to retain the *nine distinct
parts*, ... 43

1. The address of the bill. It is addressed to the
Chancellor, and in the United States, to the court
before which suit is brought, by its proper designation, ... 43

2. The introduction contains the name and abode of
the plaintiff; and in the courts of the United
States, an averment of the citizenship of both
parties, plaintiffs and defendants, . . . 43

3. The premises contain a narrative of the facts of
the plaintiff's case, ... 44

4. The charge of confederacy. No good reason for
its use. In the Federal Courts of the Union it
may be omitted, ... 44

5. The charging part states and avoids the supposed
defense of the defendant, but it is not necessary, 45

6. The averment of jurisdiction seems equally nugatory with the clause of confederacy, . . 45

7. The interrogating part prays that the parties may
answer to the best of their knowledge, information and belief, ... 46

In this part, all necessary *specific interrogatories* should
be preferred, ... 46

Rules of the Supreme Court of the United States on
interrogatories, ... 47

8. The prayer for relief may be special or general, 47

The rules of the Supreme Court of the United States
direct the plaintiff to ask for *special* relief, . 48

ANALYTICAL TABLE. 11

9. The prayer of process prays the writ of subpena, 48

It is presumed that in the United States, generally, the subpena issues *of course*, ... 49

All persons interested in the subject-matter should be made parties, ... 49

Exceptions to this rule, ... 49, 50

The objection of a want of proper parties may be made at any time, ... 50

Bill is signed by counsel to prevent scandal, . . 50

A bill, which seeks to remove a cause from the cognizance of a court of law, or which requires a court of equity to act *ex parte*, must be supported by affidavit, ... 50

A form *in extenso* of an original bill with all its parts, 51

The same bill framed in accordance with the rules of the Supreme Court of the United States, . 56

Various forms of the commencement of bills by particular parties, ... 59, 60

1. To restrain proceedings at law, and for an injunction, ... 60

Form of a writ of injunction, . . . [*note*] 60

2. For an account of the rents and profits of a testator's real estate, ... 61

3. For an account of money had and received, . 62

4. For the production of deeds and papers, . 62

5. For an account of personal estate, . . . 62

6. For a *ne exeat*, ... 63

Form of a writ of *ne exeat*, . . . [*note*] 63

7. In suits against the United States or a State, . 64

8. In suits against a corporation, ... 64

Form of affidavit to a bill, ... 64

Form of a bill to foreclose a mortgage, . . . 65

A mortgage foreclosed in this country by a *sale* of
the land, ... [*note*] 65
Form of a bill for *specific performance* of a contract
to convey real estate, ... 66
Bill for an account of partnership dealings, for a re-
ceiver, and an injunction, ... 68
Purpose of a *bill* of *interpleader,* 70
Must be verified by affidavit, ... 70
Must offer to bring the money or property into
court, ... 71
Form of a *bill* of *interpleader,* 71
This bill not applicable in cases of *bailment,* the rem-
edy being at law, ... [*note*] 70
A *bill* of *certiorari* is used to remove a case from an
inferior to a superior court, ... 73
A description of it, ... 74
Form of the writ of *certiorari,* . . [*note*] 74
Purpose and description of a bill to perpetuate the
testimony of witnesses, ... 75
Of the nature and requisites of a bill of discovery, 76
When an affidavit is necessary, ... 76
A form of a bill of discovery, ... 77
An *information* is exhibited by the attorney or solici-
tor general, and differs very little from a bill, . 78

CHAPTER II.

OF APPEARANCE TO SUIT IN EQUITY.

On the filing of the bill, the *subpena* issues, commanding the defendant's appearance,	80
In the Supreme Court of the United States it issues before filing the bill,	80
This writ vehemently opposed by the courts of law,	80
Security was formerly required of the plaintiff,	80
The form of the writ of subpena,	80
The *label*, an abstract of the subpena, is given to each of the defendants, except the last, who receives the writ itself,	82
It is rarely used in the United States,	82
If defendant is a peer, a *letter missive* issues,	82
The form of a *letter missive*,	83
Lord Bacon introduced this polite method, [*note*]	83
By the rules of the Supreme Court of the United States, a copy of the subpena is delivered to the defendant, or left at his house,	84
The writ, when against an infant, is served on the infant himself, with a notice to guardian,	84
Court may order other modes of service to be deemed good, under special circumstances,	84
Quære whether service of the writ in a foreign country is good, [*note*]	85
If writ is served, *compulsory process* may be awarded, if defendant is in contempt,	86
Modern practice usually provides for a decree *pro confesso*, if defendant neglects to appear,	86
An *attachment*, the first compulsory process,	87

ANALYTICAL TABLE.

It is in the nature of a *capias* at common law,	87
The form of an attachment in chancery,	87
In what an attachment differs from a *capias*, [*note*]	87
An attachment not executed on members of parliament or infants, ... [*note*]	88
On return of *non est inventus*, an *attachment* with *proclamation* issues,	88
Form of this writ,	89
If this writ also be returned *non est inventus*, a *commission of rebellion* is awarded,	89
The form of this writ,	90
If the commission be ineffectual, the court, on motion, will dispatch a *sergeant-at-arms*,	91
If defendant be taken, he is sent to prison until he clears his contempt,	91
But if he eludes the *sergeant-at-arms*, a *sequestration* issues, on motion, to seize his personal estate and the rents and profits of his real estate,	91
Form of a writ of sequestration,	91
This writ first used in the reign of Elizabeth, to enforce the *decrees* of the court, . . [*note*]	91
But afterward used as *mesne process*, . . [*note*]	91
A case illustrating the chain of process. . [*note*]	93
A *distringas* is the compulsory process against a *corporation*,	94
The form of a *distringas*,	94
If corporation continue in contempt, an *alias* and a *pluries distringas* issue, and finally a sequestration,	94
After an order for sequestration, the plaintiff's bill is taken *pro confesso*,	94
The sequestration answers to the *primum decretum* of the Roman law, and the *quantum damnificatus* of the common law,	96

It is the plaintiff's only remedy if the defendant absolutely refuse to appear, except when modern practice allows a decree *pro confesso*, . . . 95

CHAPTER III.

OF DEFENSE TO A SUIT IN EQUITY.

Defense may be made by *disclaimer, demurrer, plea, answer*, and *cross bill*, ... 98
A disclaimer is a renunciation of all interest, . . 98
Form of a simple disclaimer, ... 99
Seldom put in alone, ... [*note*] 99
A *demurrer* lies for defects on the face of the bill, . 100
A defendant, without a demurrer, may insist on the objections covered by it at the hearing, . . 100
The use of a demurrer, ... 100
A demurrer should be *certain*, ... 100
In England, if a bill prays discovery and relief, a demurrer, which is good to the relief, will be so to the discovery, ... 101
Aliter, in the Federal Courts and New York, . . 101
The principal grounds of a demurrer to relief enumerated, ... 101
The principal grounds of a demurrer to discovery enumerated, ... 103
Form of a demurrer for want of equity, . . 103
Forms, for want of privity, for multifariousness, and for want of parties, ... 104
Form of demurrer to a bill of discovery, where defendant could be examined as a witness, . . 104

Form of a demurrer coupled with an answer, . .
In the Federal Courts, a demurrer must be supported
   by affidavit, ... 106
A *plea* is a special answer relying on some one general fact not apparent on the face of the bill, . . 107
Classes of pleas.—1. To the jurisdiction, . . 107
               2. To the person of plaintiff, . 108
               3. To the bill or frame of the bill, 108
               4. Pleas in bar, by statute, record or matters *in pais*, . . 108
Form of a plea of another bill pending, . . . 109
Forms of a plea of infancy, and a plea of coverture, 110
Description and purport of an *answer*, . . . 111
Form of an answer, ... 112
Forms of titles of answers by particular parties, . 113
Forms of commencements and conclusions of answers, ... 114
The answer must be sworn to by defendant, . . 115
The answer of a corporation is put in under their common seal, ... 115
An infant answers by a *guardian ad litem*, and, on majority, has a day in court, ... 115
On defense by a *cross bill*, and its nature, . . . 115
Form of cross bill in the nature of a plea *puis darrien continuance*, ... 116
Form of a *dedimus potestatem* in chancery to take the defendant's plea, answer, or demurrer, when he lives more than twenty miles from London, . . 118
On filing the answer, the plaintiff may set the cause down for hearing, or he may file *exceptions*, . . 119

CHAPTER IV.

EXCEPTIONS TO ANSWER.

If the answer be defective, it may be objected to by exceptions, ... 120
No exception to infant's answer, ... 121
Form of exceptions to answer, ... 121
If defendant admits their propriety, he must put in a further answer, ... 122
If he does not, the proceedings are referred to a *Master in Chancery*, ... 122
If a defendant is dissatisfied with master's report, he may file exceptions to it, ... 122
Form of such exceptions, ... 122
If defendant persist in an evasive answer, bill may be taken *pro confesso*, ... 123

CHAPTER V.

INTERLOCUTORY PROCEEDINGS.

Interlocutory applications are by motion or by petition, ... 124
The most usual interlocutory orders relate to amendments of the pleadings; the appointment of a receiver; the payment of money into court, or references to a master, ... 124
The court may grant leave, as of course, to amend the bill before issue, ... 124

The rule is more strict as to answer or plea, . . 125
The court will appoint a receiver, to prevent waste or fraud, ... 125
The application must be supported by affidavit, if made before answer, ... 125
Defendant will be ordered to pay money into court when balance appears due, ... 126
References to a master, numerous and useful, . 126
Masters in chancery may take an account; may investigate title; may sell property, etc. . . 126
The form of an order for the production of papers before hearing, ... 127
The form of an order that the plaintiff elect to proceed at law or in chancery, ... 127
The form of an order to pay money into court, . 127
An order of reference to a master to appoint a receiver, ... 128

CHAPTER VI.

OF REPLICATION AND REJOINDER.

Ancient practice in respect to the pleading after the answer, ... 129
Special replications are out of use, . . . 129
Form of a general replication to the answer, . 130
Form of a special replication, ... 130
On filing the replication, the plaintiff serves the defendant with a subpena to rejoin, . . . 131
In the United States generally, the pleadings terminate with a replication, ... 131
The form of a rejoinder, ... 132

CHAPTER VII.

INTERLOCUTORY BILLS.

Auxiliary bills only requisite after issue joined,	133
Before issue, the bill may be amended,	133
Character of a *supplemental bill*,	133
A *bill of revivor* is used when suit abates,	134
Remarks on the use of this bill,	134
The form of a bill of revivor against the heir of a deceased mortgagor,	135
Character of an *original bill in the nature of a bill of revivor*,	137
Character of an original bill, in the nature of a supplemental bill,	137

CHAPTER VIII.

OF THE EXAMINATION OF WITNESSES.

The English practice greatly modified in the United States, [*note*]	139
The mode of examining witnesses in equity agrees with the practice of the civil law,	139
If the witness lives within twenty miles of London, the court appoints an examiner,	139
If he lives beyond that distance, *dedimus potestatem* is granted to four commissioners,	139
Form of a commission to examine witnesses,	140

After due notice, *interrogatories* are exhibited to the witnesses, and their answer reduced to writing, 141
Form of interrogatories exhibited in equity, . . 141
Form of the depositions by commission, . . 143
Form of depositions before an examiner, . . 144
The depositions are sealed and sent to court by a sworn messenger, ... 145
The competency or credibility of the witnesses may be excepted to, ... 145
Form of articles of exception to the credit of a witness, ... 146

CHAPTER IX.

OF THE HEARING OF A CAUSE IN EQUITY.

A cause may be set for hearing at the instance of either party, ... 148
A subpena to hear judgment is served when the cause is set down, ... 148
Form of this subpena, ... 148
The party has until the third day after the return of the writ to appear, ... 149
Blackstone's reason for this indulgence, . . 149
If defendant is a *body corporate*, a writ of distringas is issued instead of subpena, ... 149
The manner of arguing the case by counsel, . 149
If defendant neglect to appear, plaintiff may have a decree, ... 150

But defendant must be served with a subpena to show
    cause, ... 150
Form of a subpena to show cause, ... 150

CHAPTER X.

OF A DECREE IN EQUITY.

A decree may be interlocutory or final, . . 152
Why the first decree is seldom final, . . . 152
Description and purpose of a *feigned issue*, . . 152
When a decree may be considered final, . . . 153
Of decrees in suits against infants, . . . 154
Of decrees *nisi* or by default, ... 154
Decrees consist of three parts :—1. *The date and title.*
    2. *The recitals.*   3. *The order,* . . · 155
A *declaratory part* is sometimes used, . . . 155
A general form of a decree, ... 156
Form of a decree *pro confesso* in Ohio, . [*note*] 156
Form of a decree by default, ... 157
Form of a decree for an account, ... 157
Form of a decree for specific performance, . . 158
Form of a decree in creditor's suit, . . . 159
Form of a decree of interpleader, . . . 159
Form of a decree of sale on foreclosure, . . . 160
Decrees are signed by the chancellor and enrolled, 161

CHAPTER XI.

OF RE-HEARING A CAUSE IN EQUITY.

Re-hearing can only be had before signature and enrollment of the decree, ... 163
The party proceeds by *caveat* and *petition*, . . 163
The petition must state the objections to the decree, and be signed by two barristers, ... 164
All the evidence taken in the cause may be read at the re-hearing, ... 164
Form of a petition for re-hearing, . . . 165

CHAPTER XII.

ON THE EXECUTION OF DECREES.

Remarks on the ancient method of compelling the observance of a decree, ... [*note*] 166
When the decree is *in personam*, the process is a writ of execution, and on its failure, a writ of sequestration, ... 166
When the decree is *in rem*, after execution and attachment, an injunction to give the plaintiff possession may be awarded, ... 166
Form of a writ of execution in equity, . . 167
Form of a writ of injunction to deliver possession of land, ... 168

CHAPTER XIII.

OF REVIEWING DECREES IN EQUITY.

Upon what occasions a bill of review is proper, . 170
This bill can not be filed without leave of the court, unless the error complained of appear on the face of the decree, ... 170
Must be brought within the period which limits writs of error at law, ... 170
Form of a bill of review in New York, . . . 171
The defendant usually demurrs to a bill for error on the record, ... 172
Remarks on bills to impeach a decree and to carry a decree into execution, ... 173

CHAPTER XIV.

OF APPEAL TO THE HOUSE OF LORDS.

Difference between the English and American practice on appeals, ... [note] 174
No appeal allowed before the year 1581, . . 174
Form of a petition of appeal, ... 175
Form of a respondent's answer to the petition. . 176
Method of proceeding at the hearing before the lords, ... [note] 177

APPENDIX.

Rules of Practice for the Courts of Equity of the
    United States, ... 179
United States Statutes relating to Courts of Equity, 216
Ordinances of Lord Bacon, ... 232

A SUIT IN EQUITY.

INTRODUCTION.

HISTORY AND JURISDICTION OF THE COURT OF CHANCERY.

NOTWITHSTANDING the difficulties which are supposed to impede the success of any attempt to determine the origin of our courts of equity, I am inclined to believe that no greater portion of industry is required for this purpose than has frequently been applied with success in elucidating subjects of equal antiquity and obscurity. But in an introductory discourse of this nature, so minute an investigation would be improper. My intention at present is merely to furnish the reader with some previous acquaintance with the nature of those courts to the *proceedings* of which his attention is afterward requested; and for this purpose a very short account of their ancient and present state will, I imagine, be thought amply sufficient.

I should probably be thought inordinately fond of antiquity, were I to endeavor to show that the equitable jurisdiction of the court of chancery derived its source from the Wittenagemote, or grand council, of the Anglo-Saxon government. It is true, there is no *direct* authority for this opinion; but it seems to be founded on fair and probable grounds of deduction.[1]

---

[1] In the few observations which the reader is here presented with, relative to the origin and ancient jurisdiction of our courts of equity, he would not readily forgive me were I to perplex him with

We are informed by the records of that period that those august assemblies, when they met to deliberate on the affairs of the nation, undertook also the decision of such causes between subject and subject as they conceived to be of too much importance, or too great difficulty, for the determination of the ordinary tribunals. When the abolition of trials by ordeal and personal combat afterward gave rise to such frequent appeals to the court as to interfere with the more immediate and important objects of its meeting, a certain number of its members appear to have been delegated for the particular purpose of discharging this inferior duty. This delegation, from the place in which it usually assembled, was denominated the *Aula Regis*.[1]

The weight and authority of the monarch who at first presided there in person, enabled him to decide each case according to its intrinsic merit, without regard to the technical forms of proceeding which had prevailed in the ordinary courts of justice; but afterward, when his increasing avocations in the affairs of government rendered it inconvenient for him to attend to these subordinate concerns, and the business of the court developed on the *grand judicier*, the authority of this tribunal be-

---

references to the various authorities from which they are extracted. It may be proper, however, to say, in general, that those upon which I have principally relied are, Glanville, Spelman, Coke, and Madox. I have occasionally found it necessary to resort to the ancient records whence those treatises were compiled; and, in digesting the materials which I met with in these several authorities, I have derived no small assistance from the ingenious work of Prof. Millar on the English government.

[1] It is worthy of remark, as an example of the invariability of human nature, and of similar causes being productive of similar effects, that a like institution was formed, and by like degrees, in many other European kingdoms. Thus, the Aulic council arose from the diet of the German Empire, and the *Cour de Roy* from the ancient parliament of France. See Millar, 328.

came more restrained. The justicier, to avoid the imputation of partiality or inconsistency, found himself obliged to regulate his proceedings, in a great measure, by the rules and precedents established in the courts of common law. When, therefore, an adherence to this maxim had compelled him, in consequence of former precedents, to give a judgment which was evidently inequitable or oppressive, the party aggrieved was naturally instigated to seek redress by an appeal to the king himself, who, as the fountain of justice, was enabled to administer such relief as the nature of the case might require.

At the early period we now allude to, when the rules of law were few and simple, and the objects of dispute comparatively neither numerous nor important, applications for this purpose were probably seldom necessary. But on the accession of William I, when the Aula Regis became the king's ordinary court baron, and by the extension of the feudal tenures drew to itself the greater part of the judicial business of the nation, interpositions of this sort occasioned by the more various instances of imperfection in the rules of the common law, to which the multiplication of suits before the justicier naturally gave rise, became so frequent as to be deemed burdensome to the monarch. They were therefore left by degrees to the decision of the chancellor, who, being the king's secretary and also registrar of the decrees of the Aula Regis, was supposed to be more particularly conversant with the nature of judicial investigations.[1]

---

[1] A similar jurisdiction appears to have been acquired by the same officer in many other nations of Europe. As a reason for this, it may be observed that when the nobility, by the prevalence of the feudal laws in Europe, became vassals to the crown, and held their fiefs by charter from the king, the power of granting those deeds became the source of great influence, and caused the chancellor, to whom, as secretary of the king, it belonged, to be considered as one of the principal officers of state.

When, from the increase of civility and refinement in the nation, the rigor of the common law began to be more sensibly felt, and consequent applications to the chancellor more frequent and importunate, the necessity of this extraordinary jurisdiction became apparent. Thus it at length arose from an *occasional* to an established and *permanent* authority. But the reader perceives that notwithstanding the frequent resort to this tribunal, it does not as yet appear to have exercised an *original*, but only an *appellate*, jurisdiction, founded on the oppressive decisions occasioned by the limited authority of the inferior courts. But as the principles of natural justice, as well as of national polity, required that an *immediate* and *direct* appeal, without the intervention of any inferior court, should be allowed to that tribunal, which was alone calculated to afford relief, we find that so early as the reign of Edward I the chancellor began to exercise an original and independent jurisdiction as a court of equity in contradistinction to a court of law.

Fortunately for the growth of this new jurisdiction, it received a considerable accession of authority by an act passed in the thirteenth year of that king's reign. By this statute the chancellor was empowered to frame new writs, adapted to the particular circumstances of any new cases which might arise. These writs, agreeably to the intentions of the legislature, were at first directed to such of the courts of common law as were thought best calculated to try the merits of the question in controversy. Cases, however, soon arose which neither of those courts, by their ordinary mode of procedure, appeared competent to investigate. When this happened, the chancellor (not averse, perhaps, to the extension of his own power) ventured to summon the parties before himself, and determine their differences of his own proper authority. Having assumed a cognizance over one sort of cases, it was easily extened to others, and

Bishop Waltham, chancellor of Richard II, under color of the before-mentioned statute, and to avoid the effect of the statute of mortmain upon superstitious uses, is said to have devised the modern writ of subpena, returnable in chancery.[1]

This process was afterward, by fictitious suggestions, extended to such a variety of cases properly cognizable by the courts of common law only, that in the two subsequent reigns we find innumerable petitions presented to the Commons against the growing jurisdiction of this newly-erected tribunal. Some trifling regulations were made, but nothing effectual was done to remedy the grievance complained of till the 15th Henry VI, when it was provided that no writ of subpena should from thenceforth be granted till surety was found to satisfy the party grieved for his damages and expenses, in case the complainant did not substantiate the allegations of his bill. By an act passed in the 31st year of the same reign, it is also declared, that "no matter determinable by the law of this realm shall be determined in any other form than after the course of the same law in the king's courts having determination of the same." But these statutes, though they curbed the excess, indirectly established the legitimacy of the court; and we find, in consequence, that in the time of Edward IV, the process by bill and subpena was become its daily practice.[2]

"This, however, did not extend very far, for in the ancient treatise entitled *Diversite des Courtes*, supposed

---

[1] See *Roll. Parl.* 3 *Henry V*. But this writ (notwithstanding the suggestions of the Commons) seems rather to have been *adopted* by Waltham for this particular purpose than *invented* by him; for it is evident, from an act passed in the preceding reign, that it was by no means an unusual process. See also Spence on Equitable Jurisdiction, Vol. I, page 369.

[2] 3 Blackstone, 53. The following extract, with which I shall close this short history I have given of the court of chancery, is taken entirely from the elegant work here referred to.

to have been written very early in the sixteenth century, we have a catalogue of the matters of conscience then cognizable by subpœna in chancery, which fall within a very narrow compass.[1] No regular judicial system prevailed at that time in the court, but the suitor, when he thought himself aggrieved, found a desultory and uncertain remedy according to the private opinion of the chancellor, who was generally an ecclesiastic, or sometimes (though rarely) a statesman, no lawyer having sat in the court of chancery from the times of the Chief Justices Thorpe and Knyvet, successively chancellors to Edward III, in 1372 and 1373, to the promotion of Sir Thomas More by King Henry VIII, in 1530.[2] After this time the great seal was indiscriminately committed to the custody of lawyers, or courtiers, or churchmen, according as the convenience of the times and the disposition of the prince required, till Sergeant Puckering was made lord keeper, in 1592; from which time till the present the court of chancery has always been filled by a lawyer, excepting the interval from 1621 to 1625, when the seal was intrusted to Dr. Williams, then Dean of Westminster, but afterward bishop of Lincoln, who had been chaplain to Lord Ellesmere, when Chancellor Lord Bacon, who succeeded Lord Ellesmere, reduced the prac-

---

[1] Though the subjects, acknowledged at this early period to be cognizable by *subpœna*, must indisputably have been exceedingly few when compared with the present extensive jurisdiction of our courts of equity, yet the authority which the learned judge here refers to can not be relied upon as furnishing any conclusive evidence of their ancient limits.

[2] Sir Edward Coke observes, seemingly with some exultation, "that in perusing the rolls of Parliament in the times of these lord chancellors, we find no complaint of any proceeding before them; but soon after, when a chancellor was no professor of the law, we find a grievous complaint by the whole body of the realm—and a petition that the most wise and able men in the realm be made chancellors; and that they seek and redress the enormities of the chancery." 4 Inst. 79.

tice of the court to a more regular system; but did not sit long enough to effect any considerable revolution in the science itself—and few of his decrees which have reached us are of any great consequence to posterity. His successors in the reign of Charles I did little to improve upon his plan; and even after the restoration, the seal was committed to the Earl of Clarendon, who had withdrawn from practice as a lawyer near twenty years, and afterward to the Earl of Shaftesbury, who though a lawyer by education, had never practiced at all. Sir Heneage Finch, who succeeded in 1673, and became afterward Earl of Nottingham, was a person of the greatest abilities and most uncorrupted integrity, a thorough master and zealous defender of the laws and constitution of his country, and endowed with a pervading genius that enabled him to discover and pursue the true spirit of justice, notwithstanding the embarrassments raised by the narrow and technical notions which then prevailed in the courts of law, and the imperfect ideas of redress which had possessed the courts of equity. The reason and necessities of mankind, arising from the great change in property, by the extension of trade and the abolition of military tenures, co-operated in establishing his plan, and enabled him in the course of nine years to build a system of jurisprudence upon wide and rational foundations, which have been extended and improved by many great men who have since presided in chancery. From that time to this, the power and business of that court and business of that court have increased to an amazing degree, till we may venture to assert that it is at length governed by one of the most perfect systems of equitable jurisprudence now existing in Europe."[1]

---

[1] The following brief sketch of the origin of equitable jurisdiction, taken from the Life of Sir Thomas More, is more accurate. The author (Sir James Macintosh) prepared it, with the advantage of all the light which has been shed upon the subject, by the recent

It remains for us to inquire what matters are cognizable in a court of equity. Accurately to describe its jurisdiction Sir John Mitford observes to be a task so difficult,

investigations of the ancient records. "The office of chancellor was known to all European governments, who borrowed it, like many other institutions, from the usage of the vanquished Romans. In those of England and France, which most resembled each other, and whose history is most familiar and interesting to us, the chancellor, whose office had been a conspicuous dignity under the Lower Empire, was originally a secretary, who derived a great part of his consequence from the trust of holding the king's seal, the substitute for subscription under illiterate monarchs, and the stamp of legal authority in more cultivated times. From his constant access to the king, he acquired everywhere some authority in the cases which were the frequent subject of complaint to the crown. In France he became the minister of state, with a peculiar superintendence over courts of justice, and some remains of a special jurisdiction, which continued until the downfall of the French monarchy. In the English chancellor were gradually united the characters of a legal magistrate and a political adviser; and since that time the office has been confined to lawyers in eminent practice. He has been presumed to have a due reverence for the law, as well as a familiar acquaintance with it, and his presence and weight in the councils of a free commonwealth have been regarded as links which bind the state to the law. One of the earliest branches of the chancellor's duties seems, by slow degrees, to have enlarged his jurisdiction to the extent which it has reached in modern times. From the chancery issued those writs which first put the machinery of law in motion, in every case where legal redress existed. In that court new writs were framed, when it was fit to adapt the proceedings to the circumstances of a new case. When a case arose in which it appeared that the course and order of the common law could hardly be adopted by any variation in the forms of procedure, to the demands of justice, the complaint was laid by the chancellor before the king, who commanded it to be considered in council—a practice which, by degrees, led to a reference to that magistrate by himself. To facilitate an equitable determination in such complaints, a writ was devised called the writ of subpena, commanding the person complained of to appear before the chancellor and answer the complaint. The essential words of a petition for this writ, which in process of time has become of so great importance, were in the reign of Richard III, as

that "those who have attempted it have generally failed." Great respect is undoubtedly due to the opinion of one whose extent of erudition in this branch

follows: "Please it therefore, your lordship, considering that your orator has no remedy by course of the common law, to grant a writ of subpena, commanding T. Coke to appear in chancery at a certain day and upon a certain pain, to be limited by you, and then to do what shall by this court be thought reasonable and according to conscience." The form had not been materially different in the earliest instances, which appear to have occurred from 1380 to 1400. It would seem that this device was not first employed, as has been hitherto supposed, to enforce the observance of the duties of trustees who held lands, but for cases of an extremely different nature, where the failure of justice in the ordinary courts might ensue, not from any defect in the common law, but from the power of turbulent barons, who in their acts of outrage and lawless violence, bade defiance to all ordinary jurisdiction. In some of the earliest cases, we find a statement of the age and poverty of the complainant, and of the power and even learning of the supposed wrong-doer—topics addressed to compassion, or at most to equity in a loose and popular sense of the word, which throw light on the original nature of this high jurisdiction. It is apparent from the earliest cases in the reign of Richard II., that the occasional relief proceeding from mixed feelings of pity and of a regard for substantial justice, not effectually aided by law, or overpowered by violence, had then grown into a regular system, and was subject to rules resembling those of legal jurisdiction. At first sight it may appear difficult to conceive how ecclesiastics could have molded into a regular form this anomalous branch of jurisprudence. But many of the ecclesiastical order, originally the only lawyers, were eminently skilled in the civil and canon law, which had attained an order and precision unknown to the digests of barbarous usages then attempted in France and England. The ecclesiastical chancellors of those countries introduced into their courts a course of proceeding very similar to that adopted by other European nations, who all owned the authority of the canon law, and were enlightened by the wisdom of the Roman code. The proceedings in chancery, lately recovered from oblivion, show the system to have been in regular activity about a century and a half before the chancellorship of Sir Thomas More.

"It must not be supposed that men trained in any system of jurisprudence, as were the ecclesiastical chancellors, could have

of jurisprudence is so justly acknowledged; and it is, probably, a fortunate circumstance for the author of the present sketch, that he is not called upon, by the nature of his treatise, to enter minutely into a subject which that learned gentleman appears to have considered with so much reluctance; specifically to enumerate every object of judicial investigation which in the words of Grotius, "*lex non exacte definit sed arbitrio boni viri permittit*," were indeed not only difficult, but absolutely impracticable. It is, nevertheless, presumed that by a proper attention to the nature and constitution of our courts of equity, and the mode of dispensing justice which there prevails, the reader will find but little difficulty to determine in any *given case* (and this seems to

---

been indifferent to the inconvenience and vexation which necessarily harass the holders of a merely arbitrary power. Not having a law, they were a law unto themselves; and every chancellor who contributed by a determination to establish a principle, was instrumental in circumscribing the power of his successor. Selden is, indeed, represented to have said, 'that equity is according to the conscience of him who is chancellor; which is as uncertain as if we made the chancellor's foot the standard for the measure which we call a foot.' But this was spoken in the looseness of table-talk, and under the influence of the prejudices then prevalent among common law lawyers against equitable jurisdiction. Still, perhaps, what he said might be true enough, in his time, for a smart saying; but in process of years, a system of rules has been established which has constantly tended to limit the originally discretionary powers of the chancery. Equity, in the acceptation in which that word is used in English jurisprudence, is no longer to be confounded with that *moral equity* which generally corrects the unjust operation of law, and with which it seems to have been synonymous in the days of Selden and Bacon. It is a part of law formed from usages and determinations which sometimes differs from what is called 'common law' in its subjects, but chiefly varies from it in its modes of proof, of trial, and of relief; it is a jurisdiction so irregularly formed and often so little dependent on general principles, that it can hardly be defined or made intelligible otherwise than by a minute enumeration of the matters cognizable by it."

be the real purpose of such an inquiry), whether it be more properly cognizable in a court of equity or a court of law.

The original institution of our courts of equity, as independent jurisdictions, was, as we have seen, to supply the defects of the common law. This priciple is still adverted to in the practice of those courts, and affords a copious source of their present authority. It extends to all those cases in which the courts of law can afford either no redress at all, or not that particular redress which equity or natural justice requires.[1] Therefore,

---

[1] Equity jurisdiction, says Lord Redesdale in his Treatise on Pleading, is to be exercised—

1. Where the principles of law by which the ordinary courts are guided give a right, but the powers of those courts are not sufficient to afford a complete remedy, or their modes of proceeding are inadequate to the purpose.

2. Where the courts of ordinary jurisdiction are made the instruments of injustice.

3. Where the principles of law by which the ordinary courts are guided give no right, but upon the principles of universal justice the interference of the judicial power is necessary to prevent a wrong, and the positive law is silent.

It may also be collected that courts of equity, without deciding upon the rights of parties, administer to the ends of justice by assuming a jurisdiction—

4. To remove impediments to the fair decision of a question in other courts.

5. To provide for the safety of property in dispute pending a litigation, and to preserve property in danger of being dissipated or destroyed by those to whose care it is by law intrusted, or by persons having immediate but partial interests.

6. To restrain the assertion of doubtful rights in a manner productive of irreparable damage.

7. To prevent injury to a third person by the doubtful title of others.

8. To put a bound to vexatious and oppressive litigation, and to prevent multiplicity of suits.

Further, courts of equity, without pronouncing any judgment which may affect the rights of parties, extend their jurisdiction—

where a person had been discharged under an insolvent law, by which his body was protected from arrest, and his property happened to be of such a nature as not to be subject to the control of a court of law, the court of chancery interfered and removed the impediments to the plaintiff's judgment. So where a lady's jointure was so circumstanced that payment could not be enforced at law, it was decreed in equity. Thus again, where substantial justice requires that a contract be strictly and *specifically* performed, a court of equity has authority to compel such performance, because a pecuniary recompense, which is all that a court[1] of law can give, would be an incomplete satisfaction; *et sic de similibus.*[2]

9. To compel a discovery or obtain evidence which may assist the decision of other courts.

10. To preserve testimony when in danger of being lost before the matter to which it relates can be made the subject of judicial investigation.

[1] From the narrow principles embraced in early times by the courts of strict law, no complaint was regarded unless the plaintiff had suffered in his pecuniary interests; and, consequently, on the breach of contract, nothing further could be claimed than reparation for the damage incurred. In a more equitable view, it appeared that every reasonable and innocent purpose of the contractors ought to be enforced, although the loss, perhaps, arising from the failure of performance could not be estimated in money. A court of equity, therefore, was accustomed to decree that a contract should be carried into express and strict execution. Millar, 482.

[2] A similar principle seems to govern the construction of mortgages and other securities for the repayment of money, and also the technical *trust* or second use, though by some writers these are classed under separate heads of jurisdiction. See 3 Blac. Com. 436, 439. The interference of courts of equity (concurrently with those of law) in cases of *partition, assignment of dower*, and *account*, may also be justified on a like principle. For, though courts of law have sufficient authority to investigate subjects of this nature, yet the established modes of proceeding by which those courts are regulated, necessarily subject the parties to great inconvenience and delay.

We may, however, remark, with Sir J. Mitford, that the courts

We have also seen that as well before as after the court of chancery had acquired an original jurisdiction, it was filled by ecclesiastics. These naturally entertained a predeliction for the *civil*, as connected with the *canon* or ecclesiastical law. They consequently adopted its rules and principles in their mode of dispensing justice; and (agreeably to the practice of that law) compelled by the oath of the defendant himself, a discovery of the facts with which he was charged;[1] hence arose another fertile branch of the jurisdiction of courts of equity, extending to every case where the facts required to support it rest solely in the breast of the defendant.

From this source, it seems to have arisen that matters of *account, fraud, accident,* and *mistake,* are said in the books to be the peculiar objects of courts of equity, a full investigation of those subjects frequently requiring a disclosure from the party himself. But it should be remarked that where this is not the case, and effectual

---

of equity, having gone the length of assuming jurisdiction in a variety of complicated cases of *account, dower,* and *partition,* seem by degrees to have been considered as having in these subjects a concurrent jurisdiction with the courts of common law, *in cases where no difficulties would have attended those proceedings in those courts.* This observation will apply to a variety of other cases at present cognizable in our courts of equity.

[1] The imperfect notions of justice entertained by our ancestors when just emerging from barbarism (a period of society at which prejudice seems to be at its height, and alternately hurries men into both the extremes of absolute insensibility and fastidious refinement), led them to imagine that it was in every case hard to oblige a man to furnish evidence against himself. This mode of examination was, therefore, wholly rejected by the common law. But the purer ideas of equity which prevailed in the later period of the institution of our courts of equity, gave rise to a mode of reasoning far more consonant with justice, viz: that if the party were innocent of the charge alleged against him, he could not be hurt by an examination; but if on the other hand he were guilty, it was irreconcilable to every true principle of justice that he should be screened from the laws by such refined notions of delicacy.

relief can be granted by a court of law, they are so far from being the peculiar objects of courts of equity, that those courts will generally refuse their assistance.[1] For want of attending to this distinction it has been incautiously said by a most able and ingenious writer, " that the court of chancery claims *exclusive* jurisdiction in all matters of *trust* and *confidence*." Whereas, various species of trusts, as deposits, and all manner of bailments, and more especially the implied contract, so beneficial and useful, of having undertaken to account for money received to another's use, are peculiarly cognizable in a court of law.

Upon the whole, therefore, the reader perceives that courts of equity, being *extraordinary* tribunals, established for the purpose of supplying the defects which the increase of commerce and social connections gradually discovered or created in the *ordinary* courts of law; he has only to consider whether the particular case which is the subject of his contemplation can or can not be fully investigated, and receive a complete and effectual decision, in the *ordinary* courts of law. If it can, to them he must resort, and in the contrary event only is he justified in appealing to the *extraordinary* tribunals of equity, which assume jurisdiction in those cases only which " are not within the bounds or beyond the powers of *other* jurisdictions."[2]

---

[1] And in one case of *fraud*, that of obtaining a will by imposition, the courts of equity will not interfere, though *discovery* be sought. 3 Bro. Par. Cas. 358.

[2] In England the chancellor is assisted in the exercise of his equitable jurisdiction by a master of the rolls and three vice-chancellors. The master of the rolls is an officer first appointed in the reign of Henry VIII, but with a jurisdiction greatly enlarged by recent statutes. In consequence of the vast amount of business in the court of chancery, an assistant chancellor was created in 1813, under the title of Vice-Chancellor of England. In the year 1841 it was deemed expedient, for the same reasons, to create two addi-

Having completed the *general* idea which I proposed to give of the leading objects of jurisdiction cognizable in our courts of equity, I now arrive at the process by which they are to be obtained.

---

tional vice-chancellors, and to transfer the equity jurisdiction of the court of exchequer to the court of chancery. There are now, therefore, five judges who preside and administer justice in the court of chancery: the lord chancellor (who is the highest judicial character in the kingdom), the master of rolls, and three vice-chancellors. These subordinate officers sit in separate courts and exercise their jurisdiction severally; yet, together with the lord chancellor, they constitute one court of chancery, in which all orders and decrees, though most commonly made by the master of rolls or vice-chancellor, require the signature of the chancellor, to whom an appeal also lies from the decisions of the inferior judges. But such appeals are, in strictness of speech, re-hearings, the chancellor being by legal fiction supposed to be present in every department of the court of chancery. The re-hearing of such appeals, and incidental applications, or motions, in original causes, constitute the ordinary business of the lord chancellor, it not being the usual practice to bring causes before him in the first instance. Since 1831 the chancellor has been relieved, except in cases of appeal, from the burdensome jurisdiction in bankruptcy, which formerly devolved upon him. A court of review was at that time established, to which was referred all matters in bankruptcy, with the qualification before expressed, consisting of a chief judge, three other judges (since limited to two), and six commissioners.

In the United States the federal courts are invested with jurisdiction in "*all cases of equity*" arising between certain classes of persons enumerated in the federal constitution. In ascertaining what is a case proper for equitable cognizance, and in directing the mode of procedure, these courts have closely conformed to the principles and practice of equity jurisprudence as administered in England. In some of the states of the union distinct courts of chancery are established, but in the greater number the same tribunal sits as a court of common law, and also as a court of equity, exercising a jurisdiction somewhat analogous to that which was formerly possessed by the court of exchequer.

CHAPTER I.

ON INSTITUTING A SUIT IN EQUITY.

A SUIT in equity is commenced by preferring to the court having jurisdiction, a bill or petition, setting forth the facts on which the claim for redress is founded, and praying such relief as the nature of the case may require. This bill or petition answers to a declaration at common law, and to the libel of the civil law. When exhibited on behalf of the government, by its proper officer, it is called an information. In ancient times, when applications to equity for relief were comparatively rare, bills were very brief and simple in their structure.[1] But as

---

[1] It may not be amiss to give here a form of an ancient bill. We copy it from the proceedings of the Record Commission. It was filed in the reign of Henry V., to compel a defendant to surrender a messuage which was the inheritance of the plaintiff, Katharine. The reader will perceive in how small a compass the whole is contained, and yet how completely it takes in the equity of the case. The bill belongs to what is called by Spence, "the obsolete jurisdiction" of the court.

"*To the Reverend father in God, the Bishop of Winchester, Chancellor of England:—*

"Beseecheth humbly your poor orator, John Bell, of Calis, soldier, and Katharine, his wife, that whereas William Atte Wode, otherwise called William Atte Downe, of Rochester, father to the said Katharine, since dead, heretofore was seized in his demesne, as of fee of one messuage with the appurtenances in Rochester—situated in the churchyard there—the which William in the feast of St. Michael, in the twenty-second year of the reign of King Richard II, since the conquest, let to farm to one Simon Stelbard, of Gillingham, the same messuage with the appurtenances, for term of seven years the next ensuing, for a certain sum to him annually to be paid; the which Simon, within the first two years, was ousted by the executors of the said William, because he would not attorn to

the business of the court, expanding with the growing wants of society, increased in quantity and importance, they gradually assumed a more technical form; until

them in the payment of the rent of the said messuage—the which messuage was since then several times alienated to divers persons, and now so it is, very gracious lord, that one Piers Savage, now occupier of the same messuage, for the which he hath not paid more than marks, hath oftentimes been required to deliver the same to the said John and Katharine—as the heritage of the same Katharine—and he hath not delivered the same nor yet will, but detains it in destruction of their poor estate and perpetual disherison of the same Katharine, if they should not obtain remedy by your gracious aid in this behalf—and the which John and Katharine are so poor, and the said John so ill, that they can not pursue the common law. Please your very gracious lordship to consider the premises, and thereupon to grant a writ to the said Piers, to appear before you at a certain day upon a certain pain, by you to be limited, to answer of the matter aforesaid, and to do right as good conscience demandeth it, and this for love of God, and in work of charity."

The following general account of these ancient bills is taken from Spence's History of Equitable Jurisdiction, vol. 1, page 367:

"The plaintiff in his bill simply detailed the facts. It was not necessary that the bill should use any particular phraseology, or that it should define or describe the cause of suit in any set or definite terms, as in a declaration at law: it was not founded on any *regula juris;* it frequently sought relief against some rule of law. All that the plaintiff had to show was, that his was a case which ought to be entertained under the powers given by the general delegation. The bills almost universally pray a subpena, sometimes a writ of *habeas corpus cum causa,* or writ of certiorari alone; sometimes for a subpena as well as one or other of those writs; in some instances a sergeant-at-arms, to bring up the defendant, is prayed for; sometimes an injunction. Some of the bills pray for surety for the peace as well as other relief; many of the bills simply ask for relief generally. In on instance the bill consists of interrogotories, upon which it prays that the defendant may be examined. The bills always conclude in terms of supplication, as, 'for the reverence of God and for work of charity,' the plaintiff sometimes adding, 'and he shall ever pray for you;' and your petitioner shall ever pray,' etc., is still appended to every petition to the chancellor. In ancient times the subpena was not issued unless the case stated in the bill was considered to warrant it, and the chancellor

pleading in equity has at length attained the certainty and refinement of a science.

Any person, whether natural or artificial, not laboring under some special disability, such as infancy, coveture, or lunacy, may institute a suit in equity. A married woman can not ordinarily sue in equity, any more than at law, without the assent and co-operation of her husband. Where, however, she claims adversely to her husband, any other person, with her consent, may file a bill on her behalf, as her next friend. In the case of infancy, any person who is responsible for costs, may institute a suit for the protection of the infant's rights, with or without his assent. An idiot or lunatic must sue by the committee to whom his estate has been intrusted.

Bills vary in their form and denomination, according to the objects for which they are exhibited. Those which bring any matter before the consideration of the court for the first time, are called original bills. Any other bills which may be filed during the progress, or even after the determination of a suit, are termed by way of distinction, bills not original. The latter class will form the subject of consideration in a future chapter, when we reach that stage in the history of a suit at which they are ordinarily preferred. Original bills are usually divided into such as pray relief from the court, and such as do not. In a general sense, every bill in equity asks relief; but those bills only are so called, in technical language, which seek for an adjustment of the matter in controversy in that suit. Bills of discovery, and bills to perpetuate the testimony of witnesses, are not considered as belonging to this class, their whole object being to obtain the means of prosecuting or defending some right, in another forum, and at a future time.

---

sometimes took the advice of some of the judges on the subject. Sometimes a letter was first written by the chancellor, urging the defendant to do justice to the plaintiff."

The ordinary form and structure of a bill in equity, though not originally prescribed by any positive regulations, has been long established by usage. The rules which have recently been promulgated by the superior courts of chancery in England, and by the Supreme Court of the United States, have introduced many changes in the ancient precedents, and if generally followed, will tend to reduce pleading and practice in equity to the simplicity and certainty of a written code.

It was formerly supposed that nine distinct parts were necessary to every bill in equity; and although some of these are now admitted to be useless, it will be convenient, in analyzing the bill, to retain the ancient division.

1. *Address of the Bill.*

In England, the bill is addressed to the lord chancellor, or other person, having for the time being the custody of the great seal. In the United States, the bill is usually addressed to the judge or justices of the court in which the suit is brought, by their proper designation. In the Circuit Court of the United States, the direction would be, "To the Honorable, the Judges of the Circuit Court of the United States, within and for the District of ―――――, sitting in Equity."

2. *Names and Address of the Plaintiffs.*

This part of the bill, which is called the introduction, should state the name, description, and place of abode of the plaintiff, and the character in which he sues, whether in his own behalf or *in autre droit*. These statements are material, both to fix the identity of the parties and to enable the defendant to resort to the plaintiff for the payment of costs, or compliance with any other order which may be made during the progress of a cause. In suits brought in the courts of the United States, it is also necessary to set forth, in the introductory part of the bill, the citizenship of all the parties thereto, both plaintiffs and defendants; for those courts have no jurisdiction unless it is distinctly shown upon the face of the bill that the controversy arises between citizens of different states.

3. *The Premises or Stating part of the Bill.*

This part of the bill should contain a narrative of all the facts upon which the right of the plaintiff to sue depends, although it is not necessary to charge minutely the circumstances which tend to establish such facts. While these statements should not be extended to an unnecessary length, as by the insertion of deeds or other writings in *hæc verba*, when the substance would be sufficient, they should be so full and explicit as to show a case proper for the cognizance of the court; and for this purpose, all the material circumstances of time, place, and manner should be averred with precision and certainty. But the plaintiff is not required to set forth any matters of which the court is presumed judicially to possess full knowledge.

4. *Charge of Confederacy.*

This part of the bill charges that the defendants, and divers other persons unknown at present, but whose names, when discovered, it is prayed may be inserted in the bill, have combined and confederated together to defraud the plaintiff of his rights. This clause, upon the general principles of pleading, would seem entirely useless and nugatory, and in the Supreme Court of the United States the rules of practice leave it optional with the plaintiff to use it or not. It is said to have arisen from a two-fold error: first, that parties could not be added to a bill by amendment, whereas, there never was a time when this could not have been done; and second, that the allegation of a confederacy would be sufficient, of itself, to sustain the jurisdiction. But as all cases of confederacy and combination, considered simply as such, appear to be equally cognizable at law, it is evident that a mere allegation of confederacy without other equitable matters to support it, could never authorize a court of equity to exercise its extraordinary jurisdiction.

5. *Charging Part.*

This part of the bill alleges the pretenses which it is supposed that the defendant will set up for his excuse or justification, and then charges other matters to disprove or avoid them. It is used for the purpose of obtaining a discovery of the defendant's case, or of putting in issue some matter which it is not for the interest of the plaintiff to admit. The introduction of this part of the bill as a distinct allegation is comparatively recent, and is wholly unnecessary in any case. It arose from a desire to avoid the delay and expense attending the use of special replications and rejoinders. The rules of the Supreme Court of the United States make it optional with the plaintiff to include this portion of the bill in either the narrative or the stating part, or to dispense with it entirely.

6. *Averment of Jurisdiction.*

This clause avers that the acts complained of are contrary to equity, and injure the plaintiff, and that he can have no relief save in a court of equity. This averment was originally intended to give the court jurisdiction of the cause; but as no assertion of this kind will induce the court to take cognizance of a case which does not come properly within its customary and established jurisdiction, it seems equally nugatory with the clause of confederacy. Courts of equity, it may be recollected, like courts of law, are guided in respect to the range of their jurisdiction by fixed and invariable bounds, founded, in some cases, on the principles and original constitution of those courts, and in others, on immemorial usage; but from which they are in no case justified in departing. In order, therefore, to entitle the plaintiff to its assistance, it is strictly necessary that he make out such a case by his bill as does, in fact, authorize the court to take cognizance of the suit.

7. *Interrogating Part.*

The bill having shown the title of the plaintiff to relief, and the proper jurisdiction in the court, goes on to pray that the parties complained of may answer all the matters therein set forth, not only according to their positive knowledge of the facts stated, but also according to their remembrance, the information they may have received, and the belief they are enabled to form on the subject. Here the bill (after prayer of process) anciently closed; this general requisition being found sufficient, it was supposed, to procure the discovery sought for. But the ingenuity of modern times having discovered the possibility of answering the terms without replying to the substance of a question, it has become necessary to prefer specific interrogatories respecting each particular fact material to be answered; and the better to guard against evasion, it is usual to direct those questions not only to the substantive fact itself, but to every circumstance which by possibility might have accompanied it. But the student should observe that as these interrogatories were introduced for the purpose of obtaining a full and sufficient answer to the charges of the bill, no other are proper to be inserted than such as expressly refer to some previous matter therein contained. But upon a general statement of a fact, every circumstance connected with it, tending to prove or disprove it, may be inquired into. It is not to be supposed that the general interrogatory in a bill is not sufficient to entitle a party to a full and explicit answer. It is, however, often difficult to make a statement with such precision and minuteness as to apprise the defendant that under a general interrogatory an answer is wanted to circumstances but remotely connected with the fact stated. Special interrogatories are therefore important to enlarge the general charge of a fact, and extend it to all those collateral and minute circumstances which, however material, the defendant may easily evade, or, perhaps, honestly suppose that he is not called upon to answer. The Supreme Court of the United States have introduced some important changes by their recent rules into the structure of this part of the bill. They have provided that no defendant shall be bound to answer any statement or charge in a bill, unless specially and particularly interrogated thereto; that these interrogatories shall be divided as conveniently as may be, and numbered consecutively—1, 2, 3, etc.; and that the interrogatories which each defendant is required to answer shall be specified in a note at the foot of the bill, which note shall be considered a part thereof.

8. *The Prayer for Relief.*

The prayer for relief is special, or general. The former is for that particular relief to which the plaintiff considers his case entitles him. The latter is generally for such relief in the premises as shall be agreeable to equity. The use of the general prayer is, that if the plaintiff in his special prayer has mistaken the relief to which he is entitled, the court may yet grant him that which his case warrants; or it may be resorted to, to extend and make more effectual the specific relief sought. It can therefore never be safely or properly omitted, being, as an eminent counsel used to say, the best prayer after the Lord's prayer. Unless the plaintiff asks for an injunction, or a writ of *ne exeat*, the mere prayer for general relief will be sufficient to entitle him to such a decree as his case requires; provided that the particular relief which is asked at the bar is authorized by the facts stated in the bill. The usual and most convenient practice is to include both prayers in the bill, first stating the specific nature of the decree which the plaintiff desires, and adding a prayer for such other or further relief as may be warranted by the circumstances of the case. This course is prescribed by the rules of the Supreme Court of the United States; and they also direct, in conformity with the general principles of pleading, that if an injunction, or writ of *ne exeat regno*, or any other special order pending the suit is required, it shall be specially asked for.

9. *Prayer of Process.*

To attain the ends of the suit, the bill in the last place prays that the writ of subpena may issue, requiring the defendants to appear and answer the matters alleged against them, and abide the determination of the court on the subject. The Supreme Court of the United States, in their rules of practice, have directed that the prayer for process of subpena in the bill shall contain the names of all the defendants named in the introductory part of the bill, and if any of them are known to be infants under age, or otherwise under guardianship, shall state the fact, so that the court may take order thereon as justice may require, on the return of the process. They have also abolished the English rule, which requires that a plaintiff who has asked for an injunction or any other special order should repeat the same in his prayer for process. Where a corporation is made defendant, the bill should pray that it appear according to law.

According to the English practice those persons only are considered as parties to a bill against whom process is prayed, issued, and served. It is presumed that in the United States generally, as in the State of New

York, the writ of subpena issues of course without any formal prayer, and that, as a consequence, the strictness of the ancient rule has been relaxed, and a person may be impleaded and treated as a defendant by a clear statement in the bill to that effect, without praying for the subpena against him.

In this connection it may be proper to add a few general observations on the subject of parties in equity.

It is a general rule that all persons who are materially interested in the subject-matter of a bill, or in the object of a suit, however numerous, ought to be made parties to it, either as plaintiffs or defendants. This rule, however, being established for the convenient administration of justice, admits of exception in cases where its rigid application would defeat the very purpose for which it was established. The following are the most important of these exceptions:

1. An objection for the want of the necessary parties will not hold where the bill itself seeks a discovery of them.

2. Nor where a person who would ordinarily be a party is beyond the jurisdiction of the court, provided that no decree is sought which would prejudice his rights; and that the merits of the controversy can be fully ascertained without his presence.

3. Where the parties are so numerous that it would be extremely inconvenient to unite them in one suit. This class of cases admits of several subdivisions: 1. Where the question is one of common interest, and one or more sue or defend for the benefit of the whole; as in the case of the creditors of a deceased debtor, where one or more may sue on their own behalf and that of the remaining creditors. 2. Where the parties form a voluntary association for private or public purposes, and those who sue or defend may be fairly presumed to rep-

resent the rights and interests of the whole. 3. Where the parties are so numerous that it would be impracticable to bring them all before the court, they are dispensed with, although they may have separate and distinct interests.

In this class of cases, however, there always exists some common right, interest, or privilege, which the bill seeks either to establish, to limit, or to take away.

As the decree of the court is only binding upon the parties to the suit, and those claiming under them, the failure to make the proper parties would be attended by all the evils of fruitless litigation, and the court is therefore always ready to hear this objection. It may be made either by demurrer to the bill, or by way of plea or answer; or it may be taken at the hearing of the cause; or the court itself may state the objection, and refuse to proceed to make a decree; or if a decree is made, it may be reversed for this defect on re-hearing or on appeal. The objection, however, is not necessarily fatal; for if there are merits, the court will allow the cause to stand over for the purpose of making new parties, and even if the bill is dismissed it will be without prejudice.

An accurate and comprehensive knowledge of the doctrine of courts of equity on this subject can only be obtained by a study of the principles which have been applied to each distinct variety of cases. The student will find these amply discussed in the larger treatises of Edwards, Calvert, and Story. The changes which the Supreme Court of the United States have introduced into the old practice will be seen by a reference to rules from 47 to 55 inclusive, contained in the Appendix.

Every bill is required (by order of court) to be signed by counsel, as a security that no impertinent or improper matter is contained therein. Anciently, the court itself is said to have perused the bill before it was filed, for the purpose of discovering whether it was framed in an orderly and proper manner; but on account of the great increase and multiplicity of business, this was afterward left to the honor of the bar. During the existence of the exchequer, however, the signature of one of the barons was always requisite before process could issue. If a bill contains matter which is impertinent, scandalous, or irrelevant, it may be ordered to be expunged, and the counsel required to pay the costs thereof to the party aggrieved.

Whenever a bill seeks to remove the cognizance of a cause from a court of law to a court of equity it should be accompanied by an affidavit of the circumstances on which the application to equity is founded. To this class belong bills of discovery, and bills to perpetuate the testimony of witnesses. Whenever any immediate order or interposition of the court is requested, as, for example, on a bill of *ne exeat*, or a bill of injunction, an affidavit is required of the truth of the bill, to protect the jurisdiction of the court from abuse.

FORM OF AN ORIGINAL BILL.

1. *The Address of the Bill.*

To the Right Honorable Edward Lord Thurlow, Baron Thurlow of Ashfield, in the county of Suffolk, Lord High Chancellor of Great Britain.

2. *The Introduction.*

Humbly complaining, showeth unto your lordship, your orator, James Willis (son of John Willis, of Babbington, in the county of Essex), an infant under the age of 21 years, to-wit, of the age of six years or thereabouts, by his said father, and next friend, and Samuel Dickinson, of, etc.

3. *The Premises.*

That, Thomas Atkins, Esq., of Taunton, of the county

of Somerset, being seized and possessed of a considerable real and personal estate, did, on or about the fourth day of March, in the year of our Lord 1742, duly make and publish his last will and testament, in writing; and thereby amongst other things devised and bequeathed as follows (here are recited such parts of the will as constituted the bequest, which was of eight hundred pounds): And that the said testator departed this life, on or about the 20th day of December, 1748, and upon or soon after the death of the said testator, to-wit, on or about the 8th day of January, 1750, the said Edward Willis and William Willis duly proved the said will in the prerogative court of the Archbishop of Canterbury, and took upon themselves the burden and execution thereof; and accordingly possessed themselves of all the said testator's real and personal estate, goods, chattels, and effects, to the amount of fifteen hundred pounds and upward. And your orator further showeth, that he has, by his said father and next friend, at various times, since his said legacy of eight hundred pounds became due and payable, applied to the said Edward Willis and William Willis, requesting them to pay the same for the benefit of your orator; and your orator well hoped that they would have complied with such request, as in conscience and equity they ought to have done.

4. *The Confederacy.*

But now so it is, may it please your lordship, that the said Edward Willis and William Willis, combining and confederating together, to and with divers other persons, as yet unknown to your orator (but whose names, your orator prays, when discovered, may be inserted herein, as defendants and parties to this suit, with proper and sufficient words to charge them with the premises), in order to oppress and injure your orator, do absolutely refuse to pay, or secure for your orator's benefit, the legacy of eight hundred pounds aforesaid, or any part thereof; for reason whereof, the said confederates sometimes allege and pretend that the testator made no such will, nor any other will to the effect aforesaid; and at other times they admit such will to have been made by the said testator, and that they proved the same, and possessed themselves of his real and personal estate—but then they pretend that the same was very small and inconsiderable, and by no means sufficient to pay and satisfy the said testator's debts, legacies, and funeral expenses; and that they have applied and disposed of the same toward satisfaction thereof; and at the same time the said confederates refuse to discover and set forth what such real and personal estate really was, or the particulars whereof the same consisted, or the value thereof, or how much thereof they have so applied, and to whom, and for what, or how the same has been disposed of particularly.

5. *Charging Part.*

Whereas, your orator chargeth the truth to be, that the said testator died possessed of such real and personal estate, to the full value aforesaid; and that the same was much more than sufficient to pay all the just debts, legacies, and funeral expenses of the said testator; and that the said confederates, or one of them, have possessed and converted the same to their own uses, without making any satisfaction to your orator for his said legacy. All which actings, pretences, and doings of the said confederates are contrary to equity, and tend to the manifest injury and oppression of your orator.

6. *Clause of Jurisdiction.*

In tender consideration whereof, and for that your orator is remediless by the strict rules of the common law, and relievable only in a court of equity, where matters of this nature are properly cognizable.

7. *Interrogatory Part.*

To the end, therefore, that the said confederates may, respectfully, full, true, direct, and perfect answer make upon their respective corporal oaths, according to the best of their respective knowledge, information, and belief, to all and singular the charges and matters aforesaid—as fully in every respect as if the same were here again repeated, and they thereunto particularly interrogated; and more especially, that they may respectively set forth and discover, according to the best of their knowledge, information and belief, whether the said testator, Thomas Atkins, duly made and published such last will and testament in writing of such date, and of such purport and effect aforesaid; and thereby bequeathed to your orator such legacy of eight hundred pounds aforesaid, or any other, and what last will and testament, of any other, and what date, and to any other, and what purport and effect, particularly; and that they may produce the same, or the probate thereof, to this honorable court, as often as there shall be occasion; and whether by such will, or any other, and what will, the said testator appointed any, and what other, executor by name; and when the said testator died, and whether he revoked or altered said will before his death, and when, before whom, and in what manner; and whether the said confederates, or one of them, and which of them, proved the said will, and when, and in what court; and that they may respectively set forth whether your orator, by his said father and next friend, hath not several times since his said legacy became due and payable, applied to them to have the same paid, or secured for his benefit, to that purpose and effect, or how otherwise; and whether the said confederates, or one, and which of them, refused and neglected to comply with such requests, and for what reasons respectively, and whether such refusal was grounded on the pretenses hereinbefore charged, or any, and which of them, or any other, and what pretenses particularly: And that the said confederates may admit assets of the said testator, come to their hands, sufficient to satisfy your orator's said legacy, and subject to the payment thereof: And that, etc. (requiring a full statement of effects come to their hands, and the disposal thereof, etc., that the plaintiff may show he has a right to the payment of his legacy, in case it should be controverted).

8. *Prayer of Relief.*

And that the said confederates may be compelled, by a decree of this honorable court, to pay your orator's said legacy of eight hundred pounds, and that the same may be placed out at interest, for your orator's benefit, until your orator attains the age of twenty-one years, and that the said eight hundred pounds may then be paid him; and that, in the meantime, the interest thereof may be paid to your orator's said father, toward the maintenance and education of your orator; and that your orator may have such further and other relief in the premises as the nature of his case shall require and as to your lordship shall seem meet.

9. *Prayer of Process.*

May it please your lordship to grant unto your orator his majesty's most gracious writ or writs of *subpena*, to be directed to the said Edward Willis and William Willis, and the rest of the confederates, when discovered, thereby commanding them, and every of them, at a certain day, and under a certain pain, therein to be specified, personally to be and appear before your lordship, in this honorable court; and then and there to answer all and singular the premises aforesaid, and to stand to perform and abide such order, direction, and decree therein, as to your lordship shall seem meet; and your orator shall ever pray:

A. MANNING.

The following form of the same bill is framed in accordance with the recent rules of the Supreme Court of the United States

To the Judges of the Circuit Court of the United States for the District of Massachusetts.

James Willis, a resident of the city of New York, and a citizen of the State of New York, an infant under the age of twenty-one years, by his father and next friend, John Willis, a resident of the same city and a citizen of the same state, brings this, his bill, against Edward Willis and William Willis, who are both residents of the city of Boston, and citizens of the State of Massachusetts.

And thereupon your orator complains and says, that one Thomas Atkins, of the city of Boston, being seized and possessed of a considerable real and personal estate, did, on or about the fourth of March, 1820, duly make and publish his last will and testament in writing; and thereby amongst other things bequeathed and devised to your orator, James Willis, the sum of eight hundred dollars ($800.00), and appointed the above-named defendants, Edward Willis and William Willis, executors of his said last will and testament. Your orator further states that the said testator departed this life on or about the 20th of December, 1822; and soon after the death of said testator, to wit, on the 8th of January, 1823, the defendants, Edward Willis and William Willis, duly proved the said will in the probate court of the city of Boston, and took upon themselves the burden and execution thereof; and accordingly possessed themselves of the testator's real and personal estate, amounting to the sum of five thousand dollars ($5000.00) and upward. And your orator further says that he has, by his father and next friend, John Willis, applied to the defendants, Edward and William Willis, at various times, since his said legacy became due and payable, to pay the same for your orator's benefit; but they have absolutely refused to pay or secure for your orator's benefit the aforesaid legacy, or any part thereof, pretending and alleging that the estate of their testator, both real and personal, was insufficient to discharge his debts, and that they have exhausted the whole of the estate which has come into their hands in paying such debts; whereas, your orator charges the truth to be that the estate of the testator was fully equal in value to the sum which was before mentioned, viz., $5000.00, and that his debts were small and trifling in comparison with that amount, and that these defendants have converted the property of their testator to their own use, without making any satisfaction to your orator for his legacy.

To the end, therefore, that the said defendants may, if they can, show why your orator should not have the relief hereby prayed, and may, upon their several and respective corporal oaths, and according to the best and utmost of their several and respective knowledge, remembrance, information, and belief, full, true, direct, and perfect answer make to such of the several interrogatories hereinafter numbered and set forth as by the note hereunder written they are respectively required to answer; that is to say:

1. Whether it is not a fact that the aforesaid Thomas Atkins did duly make and publish his last will and testament, and therein bequeathed to your orator a legacy of eight hundred dollars ($800.00)?

2. Whether it is not a fact that the said Thomas Atkins, in said last will and testament, appointed them, the said William Willis and Edward Willis, to be executors of the same?

3. Whether it is not a fact that the said testator died without revoking said last will and testament, but in fact leaving the same in full force?

4. Whether it is not a fact that the said defendants, or

one of them, proved the said will in the probate court of the city of Boston, in due form of law, and took upon themselves the execution thereof?

5. Whether it is not a fact that they have possessed themselves of the real and personal estate, goods, chattels, and effects of the said Thomas Atkins, deceased?

6. Whether it is not a fact that assets of said testator have come into their hands more than sufficient to discharge his just debts?

7. Whether it is not a fact that they, and each of them, have refused to pay the legacy bequeathed to your orator, and that it yet remains wholly unpaid?

Your orator prays that the said defendants may be compelled to render a full and perfect account of the estate, goods, chattels, and effects of the said Thomas Atkins, deceased, the value thereof, the debts due by said decedent, and to whom they have been paid or are payable, the debts due to said testator, and which of the same have been paid to said executors, and all other matters and things concerning the condition of said estate. And that this they may do upon their corporal oaths, to the best of their respective knowledge, information, and belief.

Your orator further prays, that the said defendants may be compelled to pay the legacy bequeathed to your orator of $800.00 by the said Thomas Atkins, and that the same may be placed at interest for the benefit of your orator, until he attains the age of 21 years, and then paid over to him. And that in the meantime the interest thereof be paid to your orator's father, to be applied to the support and maintenance of your orator. And that your orator shall have generally such other and further relief as the nature of his case may require.

Therefore, will your honors grant unto your orator the writ of subpena, issuing out of and under the seal of this court, to be directed to said defendants, Edward

Willis and William Willis, commanding them, and each of them, by a certain day, and under a certain penalty, therein inserted, to appear before your honors, in the circuit court of ―――― and then and there answer the premises, and abide the order and decree of the court.

J. PENDLETON, *Sol'r for Pl'ff.*

NOTE.—The defendant Edward Willis and the defendant William Willis are each required to answer the interrogatories numbered, respectively, 1, 2, 3, 4, 5, 6, 7.

COMMENCEMENT OF BILLS.[1]

Bill by a Married Woman, suing by her next friend.

Complaining showeth unto your honor, your oratrix I. B., the wife of A. B. of, etc., by C. D., her next friend. That, etc.

By Husband and Wife.

Complaining show unto your honor, your orator and oratrix, A. B., of, etc., and E., his wife.

By a Corporation.

Complaining show unto your honor, your orators, the mayor, alderman and commonalty of the city of A.

Bill by a Lunatic, suing by his Committee.

Complaining shows unto your honor, your orators, A. B., of, etc., and C. D., of, etc. (against whom a commission of lunacy has lately been awarded and issued, which is now in force, and under which said commission the said C. D. was duly found and declared to be a lunatic; and your orator, A. B., appointed committee of his person and estate.) That, etc.

---

[1] We have borrowed from Barbour's valuable Treatise on Chancery Practice the most common forms of the commencement and prayers in original bills.

By Creditors, Legatees, etc., on behalf of themselves and other persons of the same class.

Complaining show unto your honor, your orators, A B., E. F., and G. H., of, etc., on behalf of themselves and all others the bond and simple contract creditors of D. C., (or legatees and next of kin) who shall come in and contribute to the expenses of this suit.

PRAYERS OF BILLS.

1. *To Restrain Proceedings in a Suit at Law, and for an Injunction.*

And that the said C. D. and E. F., their counselors, attorneys, or agents, may be restrained by an injunction issuing out of this court from proceeding further against your orator, in the said action commenced against him in the supreme court of this state, and now pending and at issue therein, for the recovery of the possession of said premises, with their appurtenances; and also from instituting a proceeding in any new or other action at law, for the recovery of the possession of said premises, or any part thereof. And that your orator may have (*prayer for general relief*). May it please your honors to grant unto your orator the writ of injunction[1] issuing

---

[1] *Form of the writ.*—George the Third, by the grace of God, of Great Britain, France, and Ireland, King, Defender of the Faith, and so forth; to C. D., his counselors, attorneys, solicitors, and agents, and every of them, greeting: Whereas, it has been represented unto us in our court of chancery, on the part of A. B., complainant, that he has lately exhibited his bill of complaint into the said court of chancery, against you, the said C. D., defendant, to be relieved touching the matters therein contained, and that you, the said defendant, being served with a writ issuing out of our said court, commanding you to appear and answer the said bill, have not obeyed the same, but are in contempt to an attachment for not appearing to and answering the said bill; and yet, in the mean-

out of and under the seal of this court, directed to the said C. D. and E. F., their counselors, attorneys, solicitors, and agents, commanding them, and each of them, absolutely to desist and refrain from proceeding further against your orator in the said action as above.

2. *For an Account of the Rents and Profits of a Testator's Real Estate.*

And that the said defendants may set forth a full, true, and just rental and particular of the real estate whereof or whereto the said testator was seized or entitled in fee simple at the time of his death; and also a full, true, and particular account of all and every sum and sums of money which hath or have been received by them, or either of them, or any other person or persons, by their or either of their order, or for their or either of their use, for or in respect of the rents and profits of the said estate or any part thereof, and whether any and which of the said estate, or any part or parts thereof, have or hath not been sold or disposed of, and at what price or prices respectively, and when and to whom, and whether

---

time, you unjustly, as it is alleged, prosecute the said complainant at law, touching the matters in the said bill complained of: We, therefore, in consideration of the premises, do strictly enjoin and command you, the said C. D., and all and every the persons before mentioned, under the penalty of two hundred pounds, to be levied on your and every of your lands, goods, and chattels to our use, that you and every of you do absolutely desist from all further proceedings at law against the said complainant touching any of the matters in the said bill complained of, until you, the said defendant, shall have fully answered the said bill, cleared your contempt, and our said court shall make other order to the contrary. But, nevertheless, the said defendant is at liberty to call for a plea and proceed to trial thereon; and for want of a plea to enter up judgment; but execution is hereby stayed. Witness, ourself, at Westminster this   day of   in the   year of our reign.

such price or prices respectively have or hath not been paid, and to whom, and if not, why not?

3. *For an Account of Money Had and Received.*

And that the said defendants may set forth an account of all and every sum and sums of money received by them or either of them, or by any person or persons by their or either of their order, or for their or either of their use, for or in respect of the said (*as the case stated in the bill may be*), and when and from whom, and from what in particular, all and every such sums were respectively received, and how the same respectively have been applied or disposed of.

4. *For the Production of Deeds and Papers.*

And that the said defendants may set forth a list or schedule and description of every deed, book, account, letter, paper, or writing, relating to the matters aforesaid or any of them; or wherein or whereupon there is any note, memorandum, or writing, relating in any manner thereto, which now are, or ever were, in their, or either, and which of their possession or power; and may particularly describe which thereof now are in their, or either, and which of their possession or power, and may deposit the same in the office of the register of this court (or the clerk in chancery for the fourth circuit), for the usual purposes, and otherwise that the said defendants may account for such as are not in their possession or power.

5. *For an Account of Personal Estate.*

And that the said defendants may discover and set forth a full, true, and particular account of all and singular the personal estate and effects of the said testator, and of every part thereof, which hath been possessed by, or come to the hands of, the said defendants, or either of them, or to the hands of any other person or persons, by their or either of their order, or for their or either of their use, with the particular nature, quantities, qualities, and true and utmost values thereof, and of every part thereof respectively; and how the same, and every part thereof, hath been applied and disposed of; and whether any, and what part thereof, now remains unapplied and undisposed of, and why; and whether any, and what part of, such personal estate remains outstanding, to any and what amount, and why; and that the said defendants may also set forth an account of the debts due from the said testator, and of his funeral expenses and legacies; and whether any and which of such debts are outstanding, and why.

6. *For a Ne Exeat.*

And that the said defendants may be stayed, by the writ of *ne exeat respublica*, from departing out of the jurisdiction of this court. And that your orator (*prayer for general relief*). May it please your honor to grant unto your orator the writ of *ne exeat respublica*,[1] staying

---

[1] *Form of the Writ.*—George the Third, by the grace of God, of Great Britain, France, and Ireland, King, Defender of the Faith, &c. To our sheriff of Middlesex, greeting: Whereas, it is represented to us in our court of chancery, on the part of Wade Williams, complainant, against Alexander Mills, defendant (amongst other things), that he, the said defendant, is greatly indebted to the said complainant, and designs quickly to go into parts beyond the seas (as by oath made on that behalf appears), which tends to the great prejudice and damage of the said complainant; therefore, in order to prevent this injustice, we do hereby command you that you do without delay cause the said Alexander Mills, personally, to come before you, and give sufficient bail or security in the sum of £500, that said Alexander Mills will not go, or attempt to go, into parts beyond the seas without leave of our said court; and in case the said Alexander Mills shall refuse to give such bail or security, then you are to commit him, the said Alexander Mills, to our next prison, there to be kept in safe custody until he shall do it of his

the said C. D. and E. F., or either of them, from departing into parts beyond this state, and out of the jurisdiction of this court, without leave first had.

7. *In Suits against the United States or a State.*

And may it please your honor, that the district attorney of the United States for the ――― district of New York (or the attorney-general of the State of New York), on being attended with a copy of this bill, may appear and put in an answer thereto, and may stand to and abide such order and decree in the premises as to your honor shall seem meet.

8. *In suits against a Corporation.*

And that the said, the president, directors, and company of the Schenectady Bank may appear according to law and the course and practice of this court.

Form of Affidavit to a Bill.

State of ―――
County, ――― } ss.

On this ――― day of ―――, before me personally appeared the above named A. B., and made oath that he has read the above bill, subscribed by him (or heard it read), and knows the contents thereof, and that the same is true of his own knowledge, except as to the matters which are therein stated to be on his information or belief, and that as to those matters he believes it to be true.

I. V., *Justice of the Peace, or Master in Chancery.*

From their frequent occurrence in practice, we have

---

own accord; and when you shall have taken such security, you are forthwith to make and return a certificate thereof to us, in our said court of chancery, distinctly and plainly, under your seal, together with this writ.

Witness, ourself, at Westminster, the   day of   in the 30th of our reign.

been induced to insert at length the form of the following bills:

Bill to Foreclose a Mortgage.[1]

John Smith, of the city of Cincinnati, in the State of Ohio, respectfully represents to your honors, that James Brown, of said city and state, being seized in fee simple of a certain tract of land, situate in the county of Hamilton, of said state, being the southwest quarter of section four, in range six, containing one hundred and sixty acres, more or less, applied to your petitioner, on or about the first day of May, 1844, for the loan of one thousand dollars, to be secured by a mortgage on the above described premises; and that your petitioner did loan the sum of one thousand dollars to said James Brown; and thereupon the said James Brown, to secure the re-payment of the same with lawful interest, by his deed, duly executed and dated on or about the first day of May, 1844, and recorded in the recorder's office of Hamilton county, in book No. 100, conveyed the same premises to your petitioner, in fee simple; subject, however, to a condition of defeasance, on the payment of said sum of $1,000, with lawful interest, on the first day of May, 1845, thence next ensuing, as in said deed will more fully appear, a copy of which, marked A, is herewith filed and made part of this bill.

---

[1] Bills for strict foreclosure are very rare in this country. The Irish practice has been generally adopted, viz., to decree a sale, instead of a foreclosure, and if the sale produces more than the debt, to pay over the surplus to the mortgagor. The practice on foreclosing a mortgage is for the chancellor, on the first hearing, to decide on the sum due, to give a day for the payment, and to decree a foreclosure and sale *nisi*, and afterwards, in term, to decide whether this decree has been performed, and if not, to make it absolute. The proceeding to foreclose a mortgage is *in rem*, to reach the pledge, and equity has nothing else to do. Thus it can not, upon the property proving insufficient, decree that the defendant pay the balance, and give execution therefor. 1 Monroe, 66.

Your petitioner further represents, that neither the sum of one thousand dollars, nor any part thereof was paid at the time stipulated in said deed of mortgage; whereby the legal estate in said premises became vested in your petitioner, redeemable, nevertheless, in equity, on payment of the principal and interest due, and to become due thereon, and that the said principal sum, and a large arrear of interest being due, your petitioner requested said James Brown to pay the same, which he has refused to do, and still refuses.

Your petitioner, therefore, prays that the said James Brown may be compelled, on his corporal oath, to answer all and singular the premises in this bill; that an account may be taken of what is due your petitioner upon said mortgage; that the premises may be sold under a decree of this court, and the proceeds applied to the satisfaction of your petitioner's debt; and that your honors may grant such other and further relief as the nature of the case may require.

Will your honors, therefore, grant the writ of subpena, to be directed to the sheriff of Hamilton county, commanding him to summon said James Brown, the defendant in this case, by a certain day, and under a certain penalty, therein to be inserted, to be and appear before your honors, at the court-house of Hamilton county, then and there to answer the premises, and abide the order and decree of the court.

J. H., *Solicitor for Plaintiff.*

Bill for Specific Performance.

J. S., of the city of Cincinnati and State of Ohio, brings this his bill against J. B., of said city and State, and says that the said J. B., on or about the first of May, 1844, was seized in fee simple of a certain tract of land in Hamilton county of said state, and which is hereinafter more particularly described; and that said J. B. entered into a written agreement with your orator for the sale of said land, which was signed by J. B. and your orator, and a copy of which is herewith filed, marked A., and made a part of this bill. The substance of this agreement was as follows: J. B. covenanted and agreed for himself, his heirs, executors, and administrators, for the consideration hereinafter mentioned, on or before the first of December, 1844, well and truly to convey, by a good warranty deed, in fee simple to your orator, his heirs or assigns, all that tract of land situate in Hamilton county, and State of Ohio, on which he was then residing, being a part of the north-east quarter of section four, in range six, being one hundred acres more or less. In consideration whereof, your orator covenanted and agreed to pay said J. B., his heirs, executors, or administrators, the sum of five thousand dollars ($5,000) in the manner following, to-wit: one thousand dollars ($1,000) on the delivery of the deed for the premises; two thousand dollars ($2,000) on the first of December, 1845, and two thousand dollars ($2,000) on the first of December, 1846

Your orator further says, that he has always been ready to comply with the terms of said agreement on his part to be performed; that on the first of December, 1844, he applied to the aforesaid J. B., and offered to pay him the sum of one thousand dollars ($1,000) lawful money, on his delivering to your orator a valid deed for the aforesaid premises, as by his agreement he was bound to do. Nevertheless the said J. B. wholly refused to do so, and still refuses. Your orator further says that he is at all times ready to pay said thousand dollars ($1,000) and perform his part of said agreement, whenever J. B. will make and deliver to him a good and lawful deed to the aforesaid premises.

Your orator prays that the said J. B. may be required, on his corporal oath, and to the best of his knowledge, information and belief, to make, full, true, and perfect answers to the following questions:

1. Whether he was not seized in fee simple of the above described tract of land.

2. Whether, being so seized and possessed, he did not enter into a written agreement with your orator at the time hereinbefore mentioned, duly to convey said premises to your orator, for the consideration above mentioned.

3. Whether your orator has not offered to perform his part of the above agreement, and particularly to pay said J. B. one thousand dollars ($1,000) on receiving a good and valid deed for the above named tract of land?

Your orator further prays, that the said J. B. may be decreed specifically to perform his said agreement, to make a good and marketable title to the above named premises, and to execute a proper conveyance thereof to your orator, pursuant to the terms of his said agreement. And that your orator may have such other and further relief as the nature of his case may require.

Bill for an account of partnership dealings between solicitors after a dissolution, and for a receiver, and also for an injunction to restrain the defendant from receiving any of the partnership debts.

To ———— etc.

Humbly complaining, showeth unto your honors, your orator, A. B. of ——, That on or about ——, your orator and P. H. W. of ——, etc., the defendant hereinafter named, entered into co-partnership together as attorneys and solicitors; your orator engaging to bring into the business the sum of $——, and being to receive one-third part or share of the profits; and the said P. H. W. engaging to bring into the business the sum of $——, and being to receive two-third parts or shares of the said profits. And your orator further showeth unto your honors, that your orator accordingly brought into the business the said sum of $——, and that the said co-partnership was carried on and continued until the —— day of ——, when the same was dissolved by mutual consent, and the usual advertisement of such dissolution was inserted in the Gazette. And your orator further showeth unto your honors, that no settlement of the said co-partnership accounts hath ever been made between your orator and the said defendant, and that since the said dissolution, your orator hath repeatedly applied to the said defendant to come to a final settlement with respect thereto. And your orator well hoped that the said defendant would have complied with such your orator's reasonable requests, as in justice and equity he ought to have done. But the said defendant absolutely refuses so to do. And your orator charges that the said defendant hath possessed himself of the said co-partnership books, and hath refused to permit your orator to inspect the same, and hath also refused to render to your orator any account of the co-partnership moneys received by him. And your orator charges that he has, since the said dissolution, paid the sum of $——, in respect of the co-partnership debts. And your orator further charges, that upon a just and true settlement of the said accounts it would appear that a considerable balance is due from the said defendant to your orator in respect of their said co-partnership dealings; but nevertheless the said defendant is proceeding to collect in the said co-partnership debts, and to apply the same to his own use, which the said defendant is enabled to do by means of his possession of the books of account, as aforesaid. And your orator charges, that the said defendant ought to be restrained by the injunction of this honorable court from collecting in said debts, and that some proper person ought to be appointed by this honorable court for that purpose. And that an account may be taken of all and every the said late co-partnership dealings and transactions until the time of the expiration thereof, and that the said P. H. W. may be directed to pay to your orator what, if anything, shall upon such account appear to be due from him; your orator being ready and willing, and hereby offering to pay to the said P. H. W. what, if anything, shall appear to be due to him from said joint concern. And that some proper person may be appointed to receive and collect all moneys which may be coming to the credit of the said late co-partnership. And that the said P. H. W. may, in the meantime, be restrained by the order and injunction of this honorable court from collecting or receiving any of the debts due and owing thereto. And may, etc.

To the class of original bills praying relief belong Bills of Interpleader.

When two or more persons claim the same debt, duty, or thing in different titles, whether legal or equitable, from another, who is in the situation of an innocent stakeholder, standing indifferent between them, the latter, if molested by a suit actually brought, or impending, may file his bill of interpleader, for the purpose of compelling the claimants to litigate their rights at their own expense, and thus protect himself from all responsibility.[1] The court, to prevent the abuses of its jurisdiction, requires the plaintiff to make an affidavit, that there is no collusion between him and any of the parties; and where

---

[1] It should be observed that in cases of *bailment*, that is, when property has been bailed to a third person by the joint consent of both the other parties, a court of equity has no jurisdiction, as in those cases, interpleader (at least in England), may be compelled at law. Both courts, however, act upon the same principle, with this difference only, that while courts of law are confined to the single case of bailment, those of equity extend to all cases to which in conscience and justice its relief ought to be applied.

money is due, to offer in his bill, to bring the same into court. The plaintiff must show that he is ignorant of the rights of the defendants, or that there is at least some doubt to which of them the debt or duty belongs. He can claim no relief against either, but only asks for liberty to pay the money or deliver up the property to the one to whom of right it belongs, and that he may thereafter be protected against the claims of each. The only decree, therefore, to which he is entitled, is, that the bill was properly filed, and that he pay the fund into court, and be dismissed with his costs. The court then proceeds to determine the controversy between the defendants, and for this purpose, either directs an action to be brought, or an issue to be tried, at law, or a reference to a master.

Bill of Interpleader.

In Chancery.

Before the Chancellor.

To, etc.

Complaining, shows unto your honor, your orator, J. R., of the city of New York, merchant, that, on or about the 26th day of June, 1821, your orator purchased of D. S., a defendant hereafter named, a certain quantity of coal, then being on board a vessel called the James, amounting to ———— cauldrons, for which your orator agreed to pay the said D. S. the sum of $1,125, and to give his promissory note for such amount, payable in thirty days from the said 26th day of June. That such coal was delivered to your orator, and he paid on account of such consideration money $100.

And your orator further shows that some time afterward, and about the ———— day of ———— 1821, F. & S. Schermerhorn, of the city of New York, merchants, caused an attachment to be sued out against one William Williams, as an absent debtor, and that afterward L. F. and D. B. caused another attachment to be sued out against the said W. W. as an absconding debtor; that warrants were issued in the usual form to W. B., the sheriff of the county of New York, who gave notice to your orator not to pay over to any person except him, the said sheriff, any property or money, of, or belonging to the said W. W.; and further, that the said W. B., the sheriff aforesaid, and G. D., the attorney of the said F. & S. Schermerhorn, and the said F. & B., apprised your orator that the coal so purchased by your orator as aforesaid, of the said D. S., was the property of the said W. W., for whom the said D. S. was only an agent or factor, and insisting, and giving notice to your orator, that he would be held liable if he paid the residue of such moneys, or any part thereof, to the said D. S.

And your orator further shows unto your honor that he made application to the said F. & S. S., and F. & B., for leave to pay over such money to the said D. S., without subjecting himself to any responsibility therefor to them, the said F. & S. S., and F. & B., which they positively refused to do. And your orator also applied to the said D. S., to relieve or secure your orator against the effect or operation of such attachments, and from any further responsibility in the premises, but he, the said D. S., has wholly refused so to do, and has commenced an action at law, in the Supreme Court of this State, to recover the balance of the said money agreed upon as the price of such coal.

And your orator further shows that he has always been willing to pay the balance of such money to such person or persons as should be lawfully entitled to receive the same, and to whom he could pay the same with safety; and he hereby offers to pay the same into this court.

And your orator further shows that he doth not in any respect collude with either the said D. S., or F. & S. S., or F. & B., touching the matters in question in this cause; that he hath not exhibited this bill at the request of such defendants, or any or either of them, and that he has not been indemnified by such defendants, or any or either of them, but merely of his own free will, and to avoid being molested and injured, touching the matters contained in such bill. Wherefore, and as your orator can only have adequate relief in this court, to the end that the said defendants may interplead, and settle their rights to the said sum of money, and that your orator may be at liberty to pay the same into this court; and that the said D. S. may be enjoined and restrained from further proceeding in the suit at law, so as aforesaid commenced by him against your orator, and that the said F. & S. S. and F. & B., and D. S., may be enjoined and restrained from commencing any suit against your orator touching the premises; and that your orator, upon payment into court of such amount, and procuring the said defendants to interplead according to the course of this court, may be decreed to be discharged from all liability to such defendants in the premises, and may have all his costs therein. May it please, etc.

Another class of original bills, praying relief are bills of certiorari.

Where a suit is insituted in an inferior court of equity, which, in consequence of its limited jurisdiction can not do complete justice in the premises, the defendant to such suit may file a bill in the superior court of chancery, praying a special writ, called the writ of certiorari, to have the cause removed to said court. The bill states the proceedings in the inferior court, so far as it may be necessary to show the incompetency of its jurisdiction, and without praying that the defendant (the plaintiff in the court below) may be required to answer, or even to appear, or, in consequence, that the writ of subpena may issue, it merely asks for the writ of certiorari. This writ (which is not peculiar to the court of chancery) is directed to the judge of the court below, and requires him to certify or send to the court of chancery the bill or plaint, and all proceedings therein, to prevent this proceeding from being used for the sole purpose of delaying justice. The court requires the plaintiff to give bond, in a sufficient penalty, to become void only in the event of his establishing the suggestions of his bill within a limited time after the return of the writ. If the evidence produced satisfies the court of the truth of its suggestions, the cause will be retained, and the bill exhibited in the court below, considered as an original bill in the superior court, which the original plaintiff may prosecute or not, as he thinks proper. If, however, the suggestions are not proven, the other party may apply for a "*procedendo,*" which is a writ directed to the judge of the inferior court, desiring him to proceed in the cause sought to be removed. This bill is rarely, if ever, used in the United States.

The conclusion of a bill of certiorari, in which only it differs materially from the general form given in the preceding pages, is as follows:

" In tender consideration whereof, and for as much as for want of jurisdiction in the said lord mayor and his brethren, the aldermen of the city of London, over your orator's witnesses, your orator is remediless there; and it being agreeable to the rules and practices of this honorable court, upon such necessities and defects of jurisdiction in inferior courts, for this high and honorable court to remove the records and proceedings thereof into this honorable court, and to proceed in this court upon the same, and all other matters and things incident thereto, may it please your honor to grant unto your orator a writ of certiorari[1] to be directed to the said lord mayor of the city

---

[1] *Form of the Writ.*—George the Third, by the Grace of God, of Great Britain, France, and Ireland, King, Defender of the Faith, etc. To the Mayor and Aldermen of London, greeting: We, willing for certain causes to be certified of and upon a certain petition or bill

of London, and his brethren, the aldermen of the said city, thereby commanding them, upon the receipt of the said writ, to certify and remove the records of the said cause, etc., and all proceedings thereupon, into this honorable court; and that your orator may be relieved in all and singular the premises according to equity and good conscience, and that the said defendants may stand to observe and perform such order and decree therein as to your honor shall seem meet; and your orator shall ever pray, etc.

The first class of original bills, not praying relief, are bills to perpetuate the testimony of witnesses.

This bill is used where there is no reason to fear that the evidence necessary to establish facts, which will probably become the subject of controversy at a future period, may be lost by the death or absence from the realm of a material witness. It is in conformity with the usage of the Roman law in similar cases. The bill should state the general circumstances of the plaintiff's case, and the matters respecting which he is desirous of giving evidence, with such particularity as may enable the parties to direct their interrogatories to the true merits of the controversy. The bill must show an interest on the part of the plaintiff, in the subject, sufficient to entitle him to the aid of the court; an interest in the defendant to contest his title; and also some ground of necessity for perpetuating the evidence, as that the matter in question can not be made

---

of complaint, before you, against Abraham Pettit and Charles Giles, Gent., at the suit of Samuel Newland, Esq., lately exhibited and now depending, command you that the petition or bill aforesaid, with all things touching the same, by whatsoever other names the parties aforesaid, or any or either of them, are or is set down before us in our chancery, truly, fully, exactly as in your custody they now remain under your seals, distinctly and to openly send immediately, and that this writ, that further thereof we may cause to be done that which of right ought to be done. Witness, ourself, at Westminster, the   day of   , in the 30th year of our reign.

the immediate subject of judicial investigation. It then goes on to pray, "that the several witnesses to the said indenture (or as the case may be) may be examined as to the due execution thereof, and the testimony perpetuated, may it please your lordship to grant subpœna," etc.

The bill of discovery forms the second class of original bills not praying relief.

Every bill, except that of certiorari, may in truth be considered as a bill of discovery; for every bill seeks a disclosure of circumstances relative to the plaintiff's case; but that which is usually and emphatically distinguished by this appellation is a bill for the discovery of facts resting in the knowledge of the defendant, or of deeds, writings, or other things in his custody or power, and seeking no *relief* in consequence of the discovery. It is most frequently used to assist the jurisdiction of courts of law, by enabling a party who prosecutes or defends an action therein, to compel the production of deeds, or of the discovery of material facts. A bill of discovery should state the matter concerning which the discovery is sought fully and precisely, the interest of the several parties in the subject, and the right of the plaintiff to the discovery. The bill must also show that the discovery is material either to the prosecution or defense of an action which has been brought, or is about to be brought at law. If the bill is for discovery only, it is not necessary to aver that the party can not otherwise establish his case at law; but the rule is different where the bill seeks relief as an incident to the discovery. A bill of discovery, properly so called, never prays any relief. Should such a bill contain a prayer for relief, a demurrer would lie, according to the modern English practice, to the whole bill. The rule which is adopted in New York, and by the Supreme Court of the United States, and which is in accordance with the ancient English practice, is more liberal, and allows to a plaintiff, who is entitled either to relief or discovery, the benefit of that part of his bill which is good. Where the bill seeks relief as consequent upon the discovery of a bond or other evidence of title, the plaintiff must annex an affidavit of its loss or destruction.

Form of a Bill of Discovery.

To, etc.

Complaining, show unto your honor your orators, A. M. and C. M., of, etc., that, by a certain instrument of assignment, dated the —— day of ——, made between J. D., of the city of New York, of the first part, and your orators, of the second part, the said J. D. bargained and sold, assigned, transferred, and set over unto your orators, the certain property, goods, choses in action and securities for money therein, and in the schedules thereto particularly mentioned in trust (*set forth assignment, etc. particularly*). And your orators further show, that at the time aforesaid there was due and owing to the said J. D., from one R. B., of the said city of New York, a defendant hereafter named, the full and just sum of $750, being the balance of an account between him and the said R. B., and the said J. D., the particulars of which account are set forth in a schedule marked A, hereto annexed, and to which your orators refer. And your orators further show that they have repeatedly applied to the said R. B. to pay them the aforesaid sum of $750, so justly due from him, with which reasonable request he has refused to comply; and having so refused, your orators were compelled to, and did commence an action at law in the Superior Court of the city of New York, for obtaining payment thereof. And your orators charge that the said R. B. hath pleaded in such suit, and given notice of a set-off in the same, and hath delivered a particular of such set-off, which, down to the date of such assignment, corresponds with the credit side of the account set forth in the schedule hereto annexed, but that such defendant hath included in the said particular three several items—one of $50.00, one of $48.00, and one of $36.00, being charges for goods delivered in the course of the month of ——, in the year ——, for which he claims credit in such action.

Whereas, your orators charge that the said R. B., at the time of the delivery of each and every of such parcels of goods so charged for as aforesaid, knew, and was well apprised of the assignment to your orators, or that he, the said J. D., had made some assignment of all his property and effects for the benefit of creditors.

And your orators have no means of proving such knowledge or information on the part of the said R. B., in the action at law aforesaid, and can only establish the same by means of a discovery from such defendant. And they are advised that they can not safely proceed to the trial of such action without a discovery of the matters hereinbefore stated from such defendant. To the end, therefore (*special interrogatory as to knowledge*).

And that such defendant may make a full and true discovery of all matters aforesaid. May it please, etc., omiting the word "decree."

We began our inquiries with a suit instituted on behalf of a citizen, which, we have seen, is commenced by bill, exhibited in the name of the party complainant. If the same suit is instituted on behalf of the crown, or of those whose rights are intrusted to its protection, it is commenced by information, exhibited in the name of the king's attorney or solicitor-general, as his majesty's representative. This, as we have before observed, differs from a bill little otherwise than in name—as will appear from the skeleton which is given below.

To the right honorable, etc.

Informing, showeth unto your lordship, Sir Alexander Scott, Knt., his majesty's attorney-general. That, etc., and his majesty's said attorney-general further showeth, etc. But now so it is, etc. In consideration whereof, etc. To the end, therefore, etc., precisely as the preceding form of a bill.

When the suit does not immediately concern the rights of government, its officers depend upon the relation of some person whose name is inserted in the information, and who is termed the relator. The relator is considered responsible to court and the parties for the propriety of the suit, and the conduct of it.

CHAPTER II.

OF APPEARANCE TO A SUIT IN EQUITY.

When the plaintiff has filed his bill, the writ of subpœna issues out of the law side of the court, requiring the defendant to appear and answer the charges alleged against him. A custom at one time prevailed in England (as it does to this day in Virginia, and probably in some other states) of issuing a subpœna before the filing of the bill, which was abolished by statute in the reign of Anne. The recent rules of the supreme court conform to the practice thus introduced. The subpœna (borrowed from the common law form of process for a witness) is supposed to have been first applied to the purpose of compelling an appearance to a suit in equity, by Bishop Waltham, in the reign of Richard II. This writ was always vehemently opposed by the courts of common law; and having sometimes, it seems, been issued on groundless allegations, it was enacted, by 15th Henry VI, c. 4, at the instigation of the commons, that no writ of subpœna should be granted in future until surety had been found to answer to the party aggrieved for his damages and costs, in case the plaintiff failed to make good the charges in his bill. This security, however, has long since fallen into disuse—a matter greatly to be lamented —and is now required only in cases where the plaintiff resides abroad, or is about to quit the kingdom. The form of the writ is as follows:

Subpœna, to Appear and Answer, in Chancery.

George the Third, by the grace of God, of Great Britain, France, and Ireland, King, Defender of the Faith, and so forth, to Edward Willis and to William Willis,[2] greeting: For certain causes offered before us in our chancery, we command and strictly enjoin you, that, laying all other matters aside, and notwithstanding any excuse, you, and each of you, be and personally appear before us in our said chancery, on the —— day of —— next (or immediately on the receipt of this writ),[2] where-

---

[1] Three defendants only (of which a man and his wife together are deemed one) are in *chancery* allowed to be inserted in the same subpena, the reasons for which, as given by Gilbert, are, that "the plaintiff may not put in an abundance of defendants, in order to terrify and vex them, and that mistakes may not be made in transcribing a multitude of names in the label;" reasons which, though adopted by subsequent writers, the reader may probably think somewhat trivial. It is in truth difficult to account for all the minutiæ of this sort which pervade our legal proceedings; few of them, probably, are sanctioned by any other reason than this: that' as some rule must necessarily be pursued, it was in most cases thought better to adopt that which happened to prevail at the time than establish a new one. In the present instance, the revenue might possibly have been adverted to.

[2] The return of a subpena may be either ordinary or extraordinary. The ordinary return is always on some day certain in Term (that is to say, one of the common return-days.) The vacations having at the original constitution of the Terms been appropriated, those of Hilary, Easter and Michaelmas for the duties of devotion preparatory to the festivals of Lent, Whitsunday and Christmas, and that of Trinity for the purpose of collecting in the produce of the earth; but the extraordinary return, which is so called because it can be had only by application to the court grounded on an affidavit of the defendant's residing within ten miles from London, may be on any day in vacation, persons residing within that distance of the court being able, it was supposed, to leave and to return to their avocations without any material inconvenience. And in those circumstances, if expedition be required, it may be made returnable immediately, which always supposes great urgency; but no *subpena* can be made returnable immediately in Term, because, every day being then a day of appearance, no such extraordinary expedition can be necessary.

soever it shall then be, to answer concerning those things which shall be then and there objected to you, and to do further, and receive what our said court shall have considered in this behalf, and this you may in no wise omit, under the penalty of one hundred pounds, and have there this writ.

Witness ourself, at Westminster, the —— day of ——, in the thirty-third year of our reign. COURTNEY.

Indorsed, "By the court, to answer at the suit of James Willis, et. al."

And upon the label, "To Edward Willis, to appear in chancery, returnable the —— day of ——, at the suit of James Willis, et. al."

The label is an abstract of the subpena, as it relates to each defendant. It is written upon a slip of parchment and annexed to the writ. It is rarely used in the United States. Where there is only one defendant, the *body* of the writ is left either with the party himself, or at his usual place of residence; but if there be more than one defendant, the *label only* of the writ is given to those who are first served, and the body reserved for the last defendant. The reason of this is that the body of the writ may be shown to the several other defendants, to whom the labels are given, as they are not obliged to pay obedience to the label unless the writ itself, under the seal of the court, is at the same time shown to them.

If the defendant is a peer or a peeress of the realm, or a lord of parliament, instead of the writ of subpena in the first instance, a letter under the signature of the court is transmitted to him, informing him of the exhibition of the plaintiff's bill. This letter is written in these terms, and is styled

A Letter Missive in Chancery.[1]

MY LORD:

It appears by a petition, a copy of which is herewith sent you, that James Willis, an infant, has exhibited his bill in the high court of chancery against your lordship, and desires your appearance thereto on the —— day of —— next. Wherefore I do, at his request (according to the manner used to persons of your quality), desire your lordship to take knowledge thereof, and to give orders to those you employ in such matters, for your appearance to the said bill accordingly.

I am,

Your lordship's humble servant,

THURLOW, C.

To the right honorable,

Henry, Earl of Cardogan.

It is to be observed that the letter missive is not a *process* of the court, but a mere *complimentary* notice, which the defendant may attend to or not, at his pleasure. If he does not appear, a subpena must be issued against him, as in common cases. This is necessary, because all subsequent proceedings to compel an appearance, are so many processes of *contempt*; founded on a disregard of the *seal* of the *court*. They can not, therefore, be awarded on the disobedience of a letter missive only, which being a mere *ex gratia* notice, can induce no such contempt.

---

[1] The practice of sending letters missive to peers, previous to the process of subpena, is said to have been first introduced about the sixteenth year of Elizabeth. Lord Bacon, chancellor, appears to have been the first who adopted this polite method of acquainting his order with the proceedings which had been instituted against them, and it has continued ever since. It is observable that a similar practice prevailed in the Roman law, where, if the defendant was *persona illustris vel clarissima*, he was cited in writing, as being more respectful than the usual mode of citation *obtorto collo*.

The mode of serving a subpena in suits in the Supreme Court of the United States, is prescribed by the 13th rule, and is in conformity to the English practice. The service is directed to be " by a delivery of a copy thereof, by the officer serving the same on the defendant personally; or in case of husband and wife, on the husband personally, or by leaving a copy thereof at the dwelling-house or usual place of abode of each defendant, with some free white person, who is a member or resident in the family."

Service of writ against an infant, is to be made upon the infant himself. The correct practice is to accompany the subpena with a notice to the parent, guardian, or some other competent member of the family, of the nature of the writ, and the intent of the service—viz: that the infant may have a guardian assigned, to appear and defend his interests. Service against a corporation is made upon one of its members, usually upon the principal officer.

These are the ordinary modes of serving a subpena; but the court will, under special circumstances, order other modes of service to be deemed good, in the particular case. This will be done as a general rule, where the subpena is proven to have come to the defendant's hands.[1]

When the subpena has been properly served the defendant is bound to appear and answer to the charges preferred against him, in the bill of the plaintiff, within the time limited by the practice of the court, or compulsory process will be awarded against him, for his con-

---

[1] The question has been very much discussed in England, though it seems still unsettled, whether the service of the subpena may not be made in a foreign country, and the defendant attached upon the strength of it, if he come within the jurisdiction. Hoffman, in his Chancery Practice, vol. 1, page 113, after an examination of all the cases, makes the following interesting remarks: "To view the

tempt in neglecting the requisitions of the subpena. Appearance is the formal proceeding by which the defendant submits himself to the jurisdiction of the court,[1] and

point more comprehensively, let the nature of a subpena be considered. This is nothing more than a notice from the court to appear. No ministerial officer is employed to execute it, but it may be served by the party or a stranger. If derived from the civil law, as appears most probable, it answers to the *citatio verbalis*. The mutations of the civil law process for bringing a party before the tribunals of justice, appear to have resulted from the natural progress of society. At first, the plaintiff might seize the defendant in public, declaring his intention in the presence of a witness, and carry him before the prætor. To avoid the disturbance which this course tended to produce, the prætor issued his citation in writing, which the party might serve upon the defendant; and in case of disobedience, he employed a special deputy to serve a process, which was called *citatio per nuntium*. Lastly, regular ministerial officers, appointed by the government, were employed for the peculiar execution of this duty. The court of chancery, in its first proceedings, is yet in the second step of this progress. As the subpena is no more than such a personal notice, the service of it does not appear to violate the sovereignty of a foreign state. The state is not sovereign if it does not give immunity to every one living within its jurisdiction, from any interference with his personal liberty, except what arises from its own laws. An arrest or detention can therefore be only warranted by those laws, and only executed by the officer of the government. But the service of a subpena is clearly distinguishable. It is, said Chief Baron Gilbert, only a notice. And it may be further suggested that the defendant's interest is most consulted by giving him a personal notice."

[1] Anciently, the mode of appearance (agreeably to the word itself), was by the defendant's actual attendance in court, where, in some cases, he was to appoint a *responsalis*, or attorney, in open court before the justices; and in those cases, no attorney could be received but one who was so appointed; in other cases, the attorney was appointed by writ, or letters patent, under the great seal, commanding the justices to admit the person therein named, to act as the party's attorney in such particular case, as "*Rex Vice comiti salutem; scias quod N. posuit, coram me R., loco suo, ad lucrandum vel perdendum pro eo in placito, etc., quod est inter eum et T. de una carucata, terra in villa de et ideo tibi precipio quod prædictum R. loco ipsius N. in placito illo recipias ad lucrandum vel perdendum pro eo, etc.*" If such writ or letters

it was at one time absolutely necessary in every case, before any decree could be rendered against him. Where the defendant did not voluntarily obey the injunctions of this writ by entering his appearance on its return, a long chain of process was resorted to, ending in a sequestration of his property, for the purpose of compelling an appearance. There were many cases, however, in which the plaintiff had no effectual remedy; as where the defendant could not be served with process at all; or where, notwithstanding the commitment of his person, and the sequestration of his property, he persisted in refusing to appear and put in his answer. To make the process of the court more effectual, there are various statutory enactments, both in England and the different United States, providing that under certain circumstances, a decree *pro confesso* may be rendered against non-resident, absconding, or contumacious defendants, founded upon the statements of the plaintiff's bill. The process for effecting a compulsory appearance has fallen into comparative disuse, since the passage of these statutes. A full description of it is, however, retained, since there may be cases in which the plaintiff can not dispense with an answer, and the right to take a decree *pro confesso* be inadequate; as, for example, upon some bills of discovery.

---

could not be obtained, the party was obliged to appear personally in court *de die in diem* till his suit was determined; but by statute (13 Edward I, chap. 10), *general* attorneys appointed for the purpose of conducting any suit or other matter indefinitely, appear to have been allowed; and in the 20th year of the same king, the chief justice and his fellow justices were especially required to appoint from every county, "*attornatos et apprenticios qui curiam sequantur, et se de negotiis in eadem curia intromittant, et alii non.*" See Glan. lib. 12, c. 1, 2 Inst. 378; 1 Reeve Hist. 169. The present easy and convenient method of conducting suits by attorneys, gradually obtained by the indulgence of successive legislatures, founded on the perpetual advancement of science and trade, and the consequent refinement of manners.

The first of these processes is an attachment, which is in the nature of a capias at common law; and is directed to the sheriff, commanding him to attach or take up the person of the defendant and bring him into court, and is in the following form:

An Attachment in Chancery.[1]

George the Third, by the grace of God, of Great Britain, France and Ireland, King, Defender of the Faith, and so forth, to the sheriff of Wiltshire, greeting:

We command you to attach Edward Willis, so as to have him before us in our court of chancery, wheresoever the said court shall then be, there to answer to us, as well touching a contempt which he, as is alleged, hath committed against us, as also such other matters as shall then be laid to his charge; and further to abide such order as our said court shall make in his behalf; and hereof fail not, and bring this writ with you.

Witness ourselves at Westminster, the ——— day of ——— in the 33d year of our reign.   ARGEN.
WINTER.

Indorsed, " By the court, at the suit of James Willis, for want of appearance" (or answer).

Label.   To the sheriff of Wiltshire,

" An attachment against Edward Willis for not appearing at the suit of James Willis, returnable in ———," etc.

---

[1] The attachment answers to the *apprehensio realis* of the Roman law, which followed the *primum et secundum decretum* upon a citation from a plebeian, and immediately after the citation itself from the prince. The subpœna being equivalent with us to the citation from the prince, the defendant is immediately *contumax* on *disobedience;* the attachment, therefore, or *apprehensio realis,* follows. It differs from the capias at common law in this, that upon a *cepi corpus* returned on a capias, the sheriff is obliged actually to produce the body of the defendant in court, or he is liable to be amerced under Stat. West. z. c. 39; but in an attachment, it is sufficient if he de-

Upon this writ the sheriff returns either *cepi corpus*, I have taken the defendant, or *non est inventus*, he is not to be found. If the defendant is apprehended,[1] he is detained in custody until he enters his appearance, and puts in an answer to the plaintiff's bill; or on his refusal an *habeas corpus* is awarded, commanding the sheriff to bring him into court, or a messenger of the court is dispatched for that purpose. A special mandate is necessary to authorize the sheriff to remove the defendant out of the county, his authority having been exhausted in taking him.

If the sheriff return *non est inventus*, an additional process is awarded against the defendant, an *attachment with proclamation*, which, besides the ordinary form of attachment, directs the sheriff to cause public proclamations to be made throughout the county, to summon the defendant on his allegiance, personally to appear and answer the charges brought against him.

---

tain the defendant in custody till compliance. The words of the attachment being only "*quod habeas ejus corpus ad respondendum ;*" and not as in the *capias*, "*quod habeas corpus ejus coram nobis ad respondendum.*" The reason of which might be, that as the purpose of the attachment was merely to punish the defendant for his contempt, its end was sufficiently answered by his imprisonment. See For. Rom. 82.

[1] It is to be observed that although the attachment issues against all persons indiscriminately, yet it is not executed upon the persons of peers or members of parliament, those persons being, for reasons of policy, privileged from every species of arrest; and the use of the attachment issuing is only for the purpose of grounding the subsequent process of *sequestration*. The same may be observed with respect to infants, upon whom the attachment, though sealed and entered as in common cases, is never served; but an order founded on the attachment is made to bring the infant into court, where a guardian is appointed to defend his suit.

The form of this writ is as follows:

An Attachment with Proclamations in Chancery.

George the Third, by the grace of God, of Great Britiain, France, and Ireland, King, Defender of the Faith, and so forth, to the sheriff of Berkshire, greeting:

We command you, on our behalf, to cause public proclamation to be made in all places within your bailiwick, as well within liberties as without, wheresoever you shall think it most convenient, that Edward Willis do, upon his allegiance, on the —— day of —— personally appear before us, in our court of chancery, wheresoever it shall then be; and, nevertheless, in the meantime, if you can find the said Edward Willis, attach him, so as to have him before us, in our said court, at the time before mentioned, there to answer to us, as well touching a contempt, etc. (As in the single attachment.)

Should this writ also be returned *non est inventus*, and the defendant still remain in contempt, a commission of rebellion is awarded against him for not obeying the king's proclamations, according to his allegiance. This commission is generally directed to four commissioners,[1] therein named, who are jointly and severally commanded to attach the defendant, wherever he may be found within the kingdom.

---

[1] The reason given by Gilbert for this process being directed to commissioners under the great seal, and not like the writ of attachment to the sheriff, is, "that the defendant is a rebel and contemner of the laws, and to be dealt with as such; and as the sheriff can not be supposed to be capable of executing all the processes directed to him in person, it may be inconvenient to trust so great a power with the deputies of his appointment, and, therefore, the court appoints its own commissioners, who are intrusted to do every thing very carefully, and are answerable to the court for their miscarriage." For. Rom. 77.

The form of this writ is as follows:

Commission of Rebellion.

George the Third, by the grace of God, of Great Britain, France, and Ireland, King, Defender of the Faith, etc., to Bamber Tyler, William Fowler, John Miller and Thomas Porter, greeting:

Whereas, by public proclamations made on our behalf by the sheriff of Middlesex in divers places of that county, by virtue of our writ to him directed, Edward Willis hath been commanded, upon his allegiance, to appear before us, in our court of chancery, at a certain day, now past, yet he hath manifestly contemned our said command; wherefore, we command you, jointly and severally, to attach, or cause the said Edward Willis to be attached, wheresoever he shall be found, within our kingdom of Great Britain, as a rebel and contemner of our laws, so as to have him or cause him to be before us, in our said court, on, etc., wheresoever it shall then be, to answer to us, as well touching the said contempt as also such matters as shall be then and there objected against him, and, further, to perform and abide such orders as our said court shall make in that behalf. And hereof fail not. We also hereby strictly command, all and singular, mayors, sheriffs, bailiffs, constables, and other our officers and loyal servants and subjects, whomsoever, as well as within liberties, as well as without, that they, by all proper means, diligently aid and assist you, and every one of you, in all things in the execution of the premises. In testimony whereof, we have caused these our letters to be made patent.

Witness, ourself, at Westminster, the ⎯⎯ day of ⎯⎯, in the thirty-fourth year of our reign.

If the commission of rebellion is returned *non est inventus*, the court, on motion to that effect, will dispatch a sergeant-at-arms in search of the defendant. The sergeant-at-arms is an officer by patent from the king, whose duty it is to attend upon the lord chancellor, and to execute the orders of the court upon those who in any respect contemn its jurisdiction.

If the defendant is taken upon any of these processes, he is committed to the Fleet, or other prison, until he enter his appearance according to the forms of the court, and also clears his contempt by payment of the costs incurred by his contumacious behavior. But if he likewise eludes the search of the sergeant-at-arms, a sequestration issues.[1] This, like the commission of rebellion, is awarded upon motion, grounded on the return of the sergeant-at-arms, and is directed to certain commissioners therein named, authorizing and commanding them to possess themselves of all his personal estate whatever, and the rents and profits of his real estates, until satisfaction is made of the plaintiff's demands, and the court shall further order.

---

[1] The writ of sequestration, though the most efficacious process of the courts of equity, was not introduced until the reign of Elizabeth, when Sir Nic. Bacon, then lord keeper, after violent struggles with the court of common law, established its use to enforce *decrees* of the court; and it was not till long afterward that it was used as a *mesne* process of the court. See 1 Ch. Ca. 91; 2 ib. 44; 1 Vern. 58. North, in his entertaining life of his relation, the lord keeper Guilford, says "that *sequestrations* were not heard of till the Lord Couvetry's time, when Sir John Read lay in the *Fleet* (with 10,000*l.* in an iron cash chest in his chamber) for disobedience to a decree, and would not submit and pay the duty. This being represented to the lord keeper as a great contempt and affront upon the court, he authorized men to go and break up his iron chest, and pay the duty and costs, and leave the rest to him, and discharge his commitment. From thence," says North, "came *sequestrations*, which now are so established as to run of course, after all other process fails, and is but in nature a grand distress, the best process at common law, after a summons, such as a subpena is.

The form of the writ is as follows:

A Sequestration in Chancery.

George the Third, etc. To Samuel Leghorne, Peter Wilkins, Isaac Jones, etc. Whereas, James Willis, complainant, exhibiting his bill of complaint to our court of chancery, against Edward Willis and William Willis, defendants; and, whereas, the said Edward Willis, being duly served with a writ issuing out of our said court, commanding him, under the penalty therein mentioned, to appear to and answer the said bill, has refused so to do, and thereupon our process of contempt has issued against him, unto a sergeant-at-arms. And, whereas, the said Edward Willis has of late absconded, and so concealed himself that the sergeant-at-arms has not been able to find him, as by the certificate of the said sergeant appears: Know ye, therefore, that we, in consideration of your prudence and fidelity, have given, and by these presents do give to you, any three or two of you, full power and authority to enter upon all the messuages, lands, tenements, and real estate whatsoever, of the said Edward Willis, and to take, collect, receive, and sequester into your hands, not only all the rents and profits of the said messuages, lands, tenements, and real estate, but also all his goods, chattels, and personal estate whatsoever; and, therefore, we command you, any three or two of you, that you do, at certain proper and convenient days and hours, go to and enter upon all the messuages, lands, tenements, and real estate of the said Edward Willis; and that you do collect, take and get into your hands, not only all the rents and profits of all his real estate, but also all his goods, chattels and personal estate, and keep the same under sequestration, in your hands, until the said Edward Willis shall fully answer the complainant's bill, and clear his contempts, and our said court make other order to the contrary.

Witness, ourself, at Westminster, the —— day of ——, in the 33d year of our reign.   ARDEN,
                                                                                       WINTER.

The sequestration is personally served upon the tenants by two of the commissioners, which is considered as a seizing and sequestering under the authority of the writ. An order is then procured for the tenants to attorn to the commissioners, who are amenable to the court for the rents and profits: This order is also personally served. Should the execution of the writ be forcibly obstructed, a writ of assistance may be sued out, directed to the sheriff of the county, and commanding him to assist the said commissioners in such execution.[1]

---

[1] The whole chain of process is illustrated in the following case. Boudinot *v.* Symmes, Wallace, 138.

The defendant, who resided in the territory northwest of the Ohio, when in Philadelphia, in the year 1796, was served with a subpena from the equity side of the court, to appear and answer the plaintiff's bill. He entered his appearance by Rawle; but put in no answer, and stood in contempt. In this situation the complainant took out an attachment to compel an answer; and was proceeding with the other process used in Westminster, namely: an attachment, with proclamations, commission of rebellion, and sequestration. But in April sessions, 1799, the practice in this case being mentioned, Iredell and Peters were of opinion that it was not necessary nor practicable to pursue the English practice; but that the bill might be taken *pro confesso*, on the return of the first attachment, *non est inventus*. But in April sessions, 1800, Chase and Peters present, it was held that such mode of proceeding was inadmissible; that until some legislative provision or rule of practice was established, the method which obtained before must be pursued. Accordingly, the decree *pro confesso* was set aside; and the plaintiff proceeded to issue an attachment, with proclamations, which, being also returned *non est inventus*, Ingersoll, after stating these proceedings, said that the next process was a commission of rebellion, which, regularly, must have fifteen days between the test and return, as all other process of contempt should have; but as it was desirable to have an order for sequestration in this term, so as that the bill might be set down for hearing, and taken *pro confesso*, which could not be until the commission of rebellion returned *non est*, and

The reader will believe that the several processes we have been enumerating, as issuing against a defendant, to compel his appearance to the plaintiff's bill, would be ineffectual against an aggregate corporation ; which, being invisible, and existing only in intendment and consideration of law, can not be served with any personal process. The method, therefore, of enforcing appearance from a corporation is by a distringas, awarded against their lands and tenements, and directed to the

---

a sequestration ordered. Har. Ch. Prac. 203 ; 3 Black. Com. 443, 444. He, therefore, moved for an order that a commission of rebellion do issue against the defendant, returnable *immediately*, directed to the marshal, etc. He said that it was in the discretion of the court, under circumstances, to expedite this process for contempt; that in this case they were merely formal, the defendant was out of the state, and would not answer; that great delay had been already incurred, and it was due to justice that the plaintiff should have the benefit of a decree by default. He cited Hinde's Prac. 122, to show that the court might order the return *immediate*.

Griffith, J. This is a special motion, and requires notice. Has Mr. Rawle had notice ?

Ingersoll. He has not; but he will not except on that account. I will answer for that; if he objects, the order shall be vacated.

Curia. Take your order; it is perfectly reasonable. The whole proceeding in these cases, as applied to the state of things in this court, is dilatory, nugatory, and expensive; it must be altered.

The commission was immediately made out, and returned *non est*. The court then appointed a sergeant-at-arms, and directed him to go in quest of the defendant. The sergeant, not being able to find him, returned to the court, that the defendant eluded his search, whereupon a sequestration was ordered.

Ingersoll, on producing the bill, moved to have the cause set down for hearing; which was done. And upon his further motion, it was ordered that the plaintiff's bill be taken *pro confesso*, and that a decree be entered accordingly; with leave, nevertheless, to the defendant to move at the next sessions of the court to set it aside upon filing an answer; and that proof of the service of this order, made before any magistrate of the North Western Territory, should be held sufficient.

sheriff of the county or place where such corporate body is resident. The following is its form:

A Distringas in Chancery.

George the Third, etc., to the sheriff of the city of London, greeting—

We command you to make a distress on the lands and tenements, goods and chattels, of the mayor, commonalty and citizens of our said city of London, within your bailiwick; so as neither the said mayor, commonalty and citizens, nor any other person or persons for them, may lay his or their hands thereon, until our court of chancery shall make other order to the contrary; and, in the meantime, you are to answer to us for the said goods and chattels, and the rents and profits of the said lands, so that the said mayor, commonalty and citizens, may be compelled to appear before us, in our said court of chancery, wheresoever it shall then be, there to answer to us, as well touching a contempt, etc. (as in the attachment). Witness, etc. ARDEN.
WINTER.

After which, if the corporation continue in contempt, there issues an *alias* and a *pluries distrignas;* and lastly, the sequestration is awarded against their lands, etc., as in other cases; with this difference only, that when the sequestration is once awarded against a corporation, it can not, as against private persons, be stayed on entering their appearance.

After order is obtained for a sequestration against a defendant, the complainant's bill is taken *pro confesso*, and a decree made accordingly; and the sequestrators proceed, under the control and authority of the court, actually to sequester the estates of the defendant, agreeable to the tenor of the writ, in order to make satisfaction for the injuries complained of in the bill. This bill of sequestration, therefore, as Sir William Blackstone remarks, since it never issues till after the plaintiff has obtained a decree on confession, seems rather intended to enforce the performance of the decree of the court, than to be in the nature of process to bring in the defendant: and it is the only remedy, by the constitution of our courts of equity, that a plaintiff has, in case the defendant absolutely refuse to appear; for unless he come in and contest the suit, the court has no authority to investigate the merits of the subject, nor can there be any proof against an absent person. The benefit of the sequestration, therefore, which answers to the *primum decretum* of the Roman law, and to the *quantum damnificatus*, or damages of the common law, is the only satisfaction which the plaintiff can obtain.

If, however, the defendant voluntarily, or upon return of either of the preceding processes, appears to the complainant's bill, he is then within a definite time (this is fixed by the practice of the court at eight days, exclusive of the day of appearance), to give in upon oath the matter he has to offer in his defense.[1]

---

[1] By the ancient civil law, where the libel was preferred to the judge, a copy was delivered to the *reus* or defendant, who was to make his defense in ten days; if he suffered this time to elapse, the *edictum primum* issued against him, and after ten days more the *edictum secundum*; after a further period of ten days, the *edictum peremptorium*; and lastly, if he still held out for the space of ten days longer, judgment was given against him on default; and these were called the *dilationes*, or times to answer. But after the establishment of provincial judges, the *dilationes* were abolished, and the *actor*, or plaintiff, upon citing the *reus*, was required to enter into surety to end his suit in two months, and at the same time to deliver a copy of his libel to the *reus*, who superscribed an acknowledgment of its receipt; after which he was allowed twenty days to deliberate whether he would yield to the actor's demands, or contest the suit; and at the expiration of these twenty days, if no defense came in, he was presumed to acquiesce in the plaintiff's claims, and judgment was given accordingly. For. 53, C. 5, Code. lib. 3, tit. 9. But at the institution of our court of chancery, the time allowed

The regulations which have been adopted by the Supreme Court of the United States on the subject of appearance will be found in rules 17 and 18 in the Appendix.

---

by the civil law being thought too long, and that by the canon law (where it was appointed at the discretion of the judge) too uncertain, the subpena or citation was at first made returnable on a day certain, in term, which (the whole term being considered as but one day in law), gave him the whole of that term to deliberate; at the expiration of which he was to put in his defense; but this being found inconvenient and partial on account of the different lengths of the several terms, and the different periods of the term at which the subpena might be served, they at length came to the general rule we have mentioned in the text. See For. Rom. 89.

CHAPTER III.

OF DEFENSE TO A SUIT IN EQUITY.

The defendant, having appeared, proceeds to defend himself against the allegations of the plaintiff's bill. This may be done according to the nature of the case—by disclaimer, by demurrer, by plea, by answer, and by cross bill. All or any of these defenses may be joined; and formerly it was necessary that each should relate to a separate and distinct part of the bill. This doctrine, however, has been abolished by the recent orders in the English chancery, and the rules of practice in equity of the Supreme Court of the United States. (See Appendix, rule 37.)

If the defendant has no interest in the subject concerning which the bill is exhibited (which is not unfrequently the case in respect to one or other of the various defendants, who, from an over-abundance of caution, are sometimes made parties to a suit), he may avoid the plaintiff's bill by

A Disclaimer.

A simple disclaimer is a renunciation by the defendant of all interest or claim to the subject of demand made by the plaintiff in his bill. It can not be used, however, for the purpose of depriving the plaintiff of his right to a full answer, where it is evident that, notwithstanding the disclaimer, the defendant ought to be retained as a party to the suit. A mere witness may avoid answering by a disclaimer; but it is otherwise with an agent, charged by the bill with a personal fraud; for the law does not permit any man to disclaim a liability.

The Disclaimer of Samuel Dickinson, one of the Defendants to the Bill of Complaint of James Willis, an infant, by John Willis, his father and next friend.[1]

This defendant, saving and reserving to himself, now and at all times hereafter, all manner of advantage and benefit of exception and otherwise that can or may be had and taken to the many untruths, uncertainties, and imperfections in the said complainant's bill of complaint contained, for answer thereto, or unto so much, or such part thereof as is material for this defendant to make answer unto, he answers and says, that he doth fully and absolutely disclaim all manner of right, title, and interest

---

[1] The form we have given is of a disclaimer only, because that alone is the defense we are at present considering; but it is rightly observed by Sir J. Mitford, that a disclaimer can hardly be put in alone, for though the defendant may have been made a party by mere mistake, having never had an interest in the subject of the suit; yet, an the contrary likewise may be the case, and he may formerly have had an interest which he has since parted with, the plaintiff may require the disclaimer to be accompanied by an answer, as to whether that be the case or not; and this is rendered still more necessary by the modern form of bills in equity, which requires a full and particular answer of the defendant, not only as to whether the facts be as charged in the bill, but how otherwise, and in what particulars, they vary therefrom, and, consequently, there is no disclaimer alone to be met with in any of the books of practice. The form we have given above, therefore, should, generally speaking, be introduced by an averment that the said defendant doth not know that he, this defendant, to his knowledge or belief, ever had, or did claim, or pretend to have or claim, nor doth he now claim, or pretend to have any right, title, or interest of, in, or to the said legacy of £800, or other the estates and effects of the said Thomas Atkins, deceased, in the said complainant's bill set forth, or in any part thereof, either by gift, grant, assignment, or otherwise howsoever, or of, in, or to any other the matters and things in the said complainant's said bill charged and set forth; nor did this defendant ever, nor now doth, intermeddle or concern himself therein or thereabout, or in or about any part thereof, in any manner whatsoever. And this defendant doth disclaim, etc.

whatsoever, in and to the legacy of £800 in the said bill of complaint mentioned, and all other the estate and effects of the said Thomas Atkins, deceased, in the said bill named, and in and to every part thereof; and this defendant doth deny all and all manner of unlawful combination and confederacy unjustly charged against him in and by the said bill of complaint, without that any other matter or thing in the said bill contained material or necessary for this defendant to make answer unto, and not herein well and sufficiently answered unto, confessed or avoided, traversed or denied, is true; all which matters and things this defendant is ready to aver, maintain and prove, as this honorable court shall award, and humbly prays to be hence dismissed, with his reasonable costs and charges, in this behalf most wrongfully sustained.

If there appear on the face of the plaintiff's bill any defect or objections which may be offered in bar of his suit, it should be presented to the court by a

Demurrer.

A demurrer admits the facts, as alleged in the bill, to be true, but denies the right of the plaintiff upon those facts, as therein set forth, to proceed and call upon the defendant to answer. It has been called an answer in law, though not so according to the common language of practice. A demurrer, which goes to the whole bill, and upon argument or otherwise, is allowed, puts an end to the suit, although the court will give the plaintiff leave to amend his bill, upon payment of costs. As the defendant, without demurring, may, in general, insist upon the same objections at the hearing, its principal use is to avoid a discovery which may prejudice the defendant, cover a defective title, or prevent unnecessary expense and delay.

A demurrer should express the grounds upon which it

is founded, with positiveness, precision, and certainty, leaving nothing to supposition or inference. If it does not extend to the whole bill it should designate the particular parts which it is intended to embrace; otherwise the court will be compelled to examine the entire bill to discover them.

A demurrer may be either to the relief prayed, or to the discovery only, or to both, and the defendant may assign as many causes of demurrer as he pleases, either to the whole bill or any part thereof. According to the present rule in England, if the demurrer is good to the relief it will be so to the discovery; if, therefore, a plaintiff is entitled to the discovery alone, and goes on to pray for relief also, a general demurrer to the whole bill will be good. The rule which prevails in the courts of the United States, and of New York, is different, and if the bill of the plaintiff is good for either discovery or relief, he will not be prejudiced by having asked for too much.

The principal grounds of a demurrer to the relief prayed, are:

1. That the case made by the bill does not come within the description of cases in which a court of equity assumes the power of decision. The nature and limits of the jurisdiction of courts of equity can not be discussed in a treatise of this character. It is sufficient to state the general rule, that it extends to every case in which the plaintiff has a right, and the courts of law do not furnish a plain, adequate, and complete remedy for its protection. Thus, if a bill should be brought for the possession of land, which is commonly called an ejectment bill, it would be demurrable; for the proper redress is at law. It is to be recollected, however, that in many cases courts of equity have assumed a concurrent jurisdiction with courts of law, as in cases of account, partition, assignment of dower, etc. A demurrer, therefore, to such a

bill, because the subject-matter of the suit was within the cognizance of a court of law, would not be good.

2. That the plaintiff, by reason of some personal disability, has no right to institute a suit; as in the case of an infant, or married woman, or lunatic, where no next friend or committee is named in the bill.

3. That the plaintiff has no interest in the subject of the bill, or proper title to institute a suit concerning it; as where an executor does not appear, by his bill, to have proven the will of his testator, or where it appears that he has done so, in an improper court, or where a plaintiff claimed under a will, when it was discovered that on a proper construction thereof he had no title.

4. That there is no privity between the parties, and that although the plaintiff may have an interest in the subject of the suit, he has no right to call upon the defendant concerning it. Thus, although an unsatisfied legatee has an interest in the testator's property, and a right to have it applied, in due course of administration, to the satisfaction of his claim, he can not, ordinarily, file a bill against the debtors of the estate for the purpose of compelling them to discharge his legacy.

5. That the defendant has no interest in the subject-matter of the suit which can lay him liable to the plaintiff; as where a bankrupt is made defendant to a bill, which is filed against his assignees.

6. That all persons materially interested in the subject of the suit have not been made parties thereto, and that the bill is therefore insufficient to answer the ends of complete justice. A demurrer, for want of proper parties, should designate them, that the plaintiff may be enabled to amend his bill.

7. That the bill is multifarious; as where it demands several matters of different natures against several defendants

The principal grounds of demurrer to bills of discovery only, are:

1. That the case made by the bill is not one in which a court of equity assumes jurisdiction to compel a discovery; as where a discovery is sought to be used in aid of criminal proceeding; or before arbitrators; or in support of an action contrary to public policy; or where it relates to facts which were communicated to the defendant in professional confidence, while he was acting as attorney or arbitrator.

2. That the plaintiff has no interest in the subject which will entitle him to call upon the defendant for a discovery; as where the plaintiff seeks a discovery, to support an action at law, and the case stated by the bill is not such as to maintain an action.

3. That the defendant has no interest in the subject-matter of the controversy, which would prevent his being examined at law, and is, therefore, a mere witness.

4. That the discovery, if obtained, would be immaterial.

The following is the form of a general demurrer, for want of equity, adapted to the original bill, which we have inserted. It may, however, be considerably abbreviated.

The joint and several Demurrer of Edward Willis and William Willis, two of the Defendants to the Bill of Complaint of James Willis, an infant, by his father and next friend.

These defendants, by protestation,[1] not confessing any

---

[1] As it was imagined that a defendant would in no case endeavor to avoid the plaintiff's bill by demurrer, when he could venture *bona fide* to deny the truth of its allegations upon oath, it very early became an established rule of judgment in courts of equity, that everything to which the demurrer extends is true. Hence arose the practice of introducing a protestation against the truth of any of the facts alleged by the bill; but it has no weight with the court, and is entirely useless.

of the matters, in and by said bill complained of, to be true in manner and form, as the same are set forth, severally say that they are advised that there is no matter or thing in said bill, good and sufficient in law, to call these defendants to account in this honorable court for the same; but that there is good cause of demurrer thereunto, and they do demur accordingly; and for causes of demurrer, say, that said bill, in case the same were true, contains no matter of equity whereon this court can ground any decree, or give complainant any relief as against these defendants. Wherefore, and for divers other errors in said bill contained and appearing on the face thereof, these defendants do demur thereto, and humbly crave the judgment of this honorable court, whether they are compellable, or ought to make any answer thereunto otherwise than as aforesaid. And these defendants humbly pray to be hence dismissed with their costs and charges, in this behalf most wrongfully sustained.

A. STAINSBY.

The commencement and conclusion may be varied so as to suit the following additional forms:

Demurrer for want of Privity.

That it appears by the said complainant's said bill, that there is no privity between the said complainant and this defendant, to enable the said complainant to call on this defendant for payment of any debt due to the estate of the said testator from this defendant; wherefore, etc.

Demurrer for Multifariousness.

That it appears by the said bill, that the same is exhibited by the said complainant against this defendant, and A. B., C. D., E. F., and G. H. as defendants thereto for several distinct matters and causes, in many whereof, as appears by the said bill, this defendant is in no way interested; and, by reason of such distinct matters, the said bill is drawn out to a considerable length, and this defendant is compelled to be put at charges in respect thereof; and by joining distinct matters together, which do not depend on each other, the proceedings in the progress of the said suit will be intricate and prolix, and this defendant put to unnecessary charges and expenses, in matters which in no way relate to or concern him; wherefore, etc.

Demurrer for want of Parties.

That it appears by the said complainant's bill, that A. B., therein named, is a necessary party to the said bill, in as much as it is therein stated that C. D., the testator in the said bill named, did, in his lifetime, by certain conveyances made to the said A. B., in consideration of $——, convey to him, by way of mortgage, certain estates in said bill particularly mentioned and described, for the purpose of paying the said testator's debts and legacies; but the said complainant has not made the said A. B. a party to the said bill. Wherefore, etc.

Demurrer to a Bill of Discovery, where the Defendant could be examined as a Witness.

That the said defendant has not, in and by his said bill, stated, charged, or shown that the defendant has, or pretends to have, any right, title, or interest in the matters and things complained of by the said bill, or any of them; or any right to call on this defendant, in a court of equity, for a discovery of said matters and things, or any of them. And that for anything that appears to the contrary by said bill, this defendant may be examined as a witness in this suit. Wherefore, etc.

Demurrer coupled with an Answer.

The Demurrer of the Defendant, C. D., to part, and his Answer to the residue of the Bill of Complaint of A. B.

(Set forth the demurrer as in any of the above forms, and proceed.)

And as to the residue of said bill, this defendant, not waiving his demurrer, but relying thereon, and saving and reserving to himself now, and at all times hereafter, all manner of benefit and exception which can be had to the residue of said bill, for answer thereto, or to so much thereof as these defendants are advised is in anywise material or necessary for them to answer unto, answer and say, that, etc.

Every species of defense to a bill in equity is required to be signed by counsel, as evidence of its propriety and sufficiency; but as a demurrer alleges no facts, but rests on matters apparent to the bill, it is not like an answer put in upon the oath of the defendant. In the courts of the United States, however, no demurrer is allowed to be filed unless upon the certificate of counsel that, in his opinion, it is well founded in point of law, and the affidavit of the defendant, that it is not interposed for delay. The rules of the Supreme Court on the subject of demurrers and pleas will be found in the Appendix, from the 31st to the 38th, inclusive.

If the defects in the case of the plaintiff do not appear, upon a mere *inspection* of the bill, the objection must be offered in the shape of

A Plea.

A plea is defined as a *special answer*, showing or relying upon one or more things, as a cause why the suit should be either dismissed, delayed, or debarred: it does not, like a demurrer, rest on the facts charged in the plaintiff's bill, but alleges other facts, to which he may reply. The office of a plea, generally, is, not to deny the equity, but to bring forward a fact which, if true, displaces it. As its object is to save time and expense, it should not consist of a variety of circumstances, unless in their combined result they establish some one general fact which displaces the equity.

The form of a plea, like a demurrer, commences with a protestation against confessing the truth of any matter. For the sake, however, of deciding upon the validity of the plea, the bill, so far as it remains uncontradicted, is assumed to be true. The extent of the plea, that is, whether it goes to the whole of the bill or only a part thereof, should be set forth distinctly. Then follow the defendant's grounds of objection to the jurisdiction of the court, the person of the plaintiff, or in bar of suit; and these must be supported by averments, so clear, positive and distinct, of every fact and circumstance essential to render it a complete equitable bar, that the plaintiff may be enabled to take issue upon its validity.

Pleas to the jurisdiction, to the person, or of any matter recorded in the bar, do not require to be put in upon oath; but the rule is otherwise as to pleas in bar, founded on matters *in pais*. Pleas have been arranged under four classes: 1, to the jurisdiction; 2, to the person of the plaintiff; 3, to the bill, or the frame thereof; and 4, in bar.

1. A plea to the jurisdiction does not dispute the right of the plaintiff in the suit, but simply asserts either that his claim is not a fit subject of cognizance in a court of equity, or that some other tribunal is invested with the proper jurisdiction. It is difficult to disguise any case which this plea would reach, so as to avoid a demurrer; but there may be instances to the contrary, and even false averments in the bill, which would leave the defendant no other means of protecting himself. If, for example, a bill in the Circuit Court of the United States should allege that the plaintiffs and defendants were citizens of

different states (without which no jurisdiction would ordinarily attach), the defendant can only contest this fact by a plea to the jurisdiction. The court of chancery being one of general equity jurisdiction, a mere allegation of the want of jurisdiction is not sufficient, but the plea must show by what means the jurisdiction has been lost, and by what court it is possessed.

2. A plea to the person merely disputes the ability of the plaintiff to sue, without putting in issue the subject-matter of the controversy. It may assert either that the plaintiff is an alien enemy; or that he is an alien, and the suit respects lands; or that he is an infant, *feme covert*, lunatic, or bankrupt; or that he is not the person whom he pretends to be in his bill; or does not sustain the character which he assumes.

3. Pleas to the bill, or the frame of the bill, bear a close resemblance to pleas in abatement of the action at common law. Without disputing the right of the plaintiff to the relief which he seeks, they allege that the suit, as it appears on the record, is insufficient to answer purposes of complete justice, or ought not for some reason to proceed. The most usual of these pleas are either, 1, the pendency of another suit for the same matter in another court of equity;[1] or, 2, the want of proper parties to the bill.

4. Pleas in bar are usually divided into three heads: 1, Pleas founded on some bar created by statute; 2, Pleas founded on matter of record; and 3, Pleas of matter *in pais*.

---

[1] The pendency of another suit for the same subject-matter in a court of law is not, however, a good plea. There are many cases in which a court of law would be incapable of ascertaining the merits of a controversy. The defendant, however, may put the plaintiff to his election whether he will proceed with his suit in law or equity; and, if the former, the bill will be dismissed; if the latter, an injunction will issue to stay any further proceedings at law.

Any statute, public or private, which may be a bar to the demands of the plaintiff, may be pleaded, with the averments necessary to bring the case of the defendant within it. The most usual pleas of this character are of the statute of limitations and the statute of frauds.

Under the second head may be included the plea of a judgment at law of a court of record between the same parties, or a final decree or order of a court of equity in a suit between the same parties, and for the same subject-matter.

To the last head of matters purely *in pais* belong the plea of a stated account, of an award, of a release, of a purchase for a valuable consideration, and of title in the defendant, obtained either by adverse possession for a length of time, or by deed or will.

Pleas to bills which are brought only for discovery, are so nearly the same as the causes of demurrer to a bill of discovery, which we have before considered, that it is not important, in this brief treatise, to give them a separate consideration.

Form of Pleas.

The joint and several Plea of Edward Willis and William Willis, two of the Defendants to the Bill of Complaint of James Willis, an infant, by his father and next friend, John Willis.

These defendants, by protestation not confessing any of the matters in said bill contained to be true in manner and form, as the same are therein set forth, do plead thereunto; and for cause of plea say, that heretofore, and before said complainant exhibited his present bill in this honorable court, to wit: on the ninth day of February, 1752, the said now complainant, together with John Willis, his father, did exhibit their bill of complaint in this honorable court, against these defendants, for the same matters, and to the same effect, and for the like relief, as the said now complainant doth by his present bill demand and set forth; to which said first bill these defendants did put in their joint and several answers, and the said complainant thereunto did reply; and other proceeedings were thereupon had; and the said former bill is still depending in this court, and the matters thereof undetermined; and, therefore, the said defendants do plead the former bill, answer and proceedings, in bar to the present bill; and humbly pray the judgment of this honorable court, whether it behooves them to make any other or further answer thereto than as aforesaid, and pray to be hence dismissed with their reasonable costs and charges, in this behalf most wrongfully sustained. A. STAINSBY.

Plea of Infancy, to a Bill exhibited without a Prochein Ami.

(For the title and commencement, see above.) That the said complainant, before and at the time of filing his said bill, in which he appears as the sole complainant, was, and now is, an infant, under the age of twenty-one years, that is to say, of the age of ——— or thereabouts. Therefore, etc.

Plea of Coverture of the Plaintiff.

That the said complainant, A. B., before, and at the time of exhibiting her said bill, was, and now is, under the coverture of one C. D., her husband, who is still living, and in every respect capable, if necessary, of instituting any suit at law, or in equity, on her behalf. Therefore, etc. (concluding as in the preceding form.)

If the plaintiff conceives a plea to be defective in point of form or substance, he may take the judgment of the court upon its sufficiency. Upon argument of the plea, it may either be allowed simply, or the benefit of it may be saved to the hearing; or it may be ordered to stand for an answer. This latter order is usually made where the plea states matter which may be a defense to the bill, though not, perhaps, proper for a plea, or informally pleaded.

The court will permit a plea which is good in substance, though irregular in shape, to be amended; but that this indulgence may not be used for the purposes of delay, it will be granted only upon condition that the party agree to amend by a very short day, and that he account satisfactorily for the occurrence of the mistake, and explain the nature of the amendment.

If there is nothing in the bill of the plaintiff to which the defendant is able or willing to *demur;* and if he have no intrinsic matter, which he can offer by way of plea; or if his plea, or demurrer, has been overruled, he may proceed to controvert the claims of the plaintiff, by

An Answer.

An answer generally controverts the facts stated in the bill, or some of them, and states other facts, to show the rights of the defendant in the subject of the suit; but sometimes it admits the truth of the case made by the bill, and either with or without stating additional facts, submits the questions arising upon the case thus made to the judgment of the court. In all cases where relief is sought, an answer consists of two parts; first, the defense to the case made by the bill, and second, the response of the defendant to the interrogatories of the plaintiff. Where a defendant submits to answer at all, he must make a full, frank and explicit disclosure of all matters material or necessary to be answered, whether resting within his own knowledge, or upon his information or belief. He can not be required to answer any interrogatories which would either lead to his own crimination, or which are irrelevant or immaterial to the case of the complaint.

Form of Answer.

The joint and several Answers of Edward Willis and William Willis, two of the Defendants to the Bill of Complaint of James Willis, an infant, by John Willis, his father and next friend.

These defendants, now and at all times hereafter, reserving all manner of benefit and advantage to themselves of exception to the many errors and insufficiencies in said bill contained, for answer thereto, or unto so much or such parts thereof as these defendants are advised is material for them to make answer unto; they answer and say: They admit that Thomas Atkins, in said bill named, did duly make and execute such last will and testament in writing, of such date and to such purport and effect as in said bill mentioned and set forth; and did thereby bequeath to the complainant, James Willis, such legacy of £800, in the words for the purpose mentioned in said bill, or words to a like purport and effect. They further admit that the said testator, Thomas Atkins, did by such will appoint these defendants executors thereof, and that the said testator died on or about the 20th day of December, 1748, without revoking or altering the said will. And these defendants further admit that they, some time after, to wit: about the month of January, 1750, duly proved said will in the prerogative court of the Archbishop of Canterbury, and took upon themselves the burden of the execution thereof; and they are ready to produce said probate, as this honorable court shall direct. They further admit that the said complainant, James Willis, by his said father, did, several times, since the said legacy of £800 became payable, apply to them to have the same paid or secured for the benefit of said complainant, which these defendants decline to do, by reason that the said complainant was, and still is, an infant, under the age of twenty-one years. Wherefore, these defendants could not, as they are advised, be safe in making such payment, or in securing said legacy, in any manner for the benefit of said complainant, but by the order and direction, and under the sanction of this honorable court.

And these defendants further answering, say: That by virtue of the said will, they possess themselves of the real and personal estate, goods, chattels, and effects of the said testator, to a considerable amount; and they admit that assets are come to their hands, sufficient to satisfy said complainant's legacy, and subject to the payment thereof; and they are willing and desirous, and do hereby offer to pay the same, as this honorable court shall direct, being indemnified therein. And these defendants deny all unlawful combination in said bill charged, without that any other matter or thing material for them to make answer to, and not herein sufficiently answered, avoided, or denied, is true to the knowledge or belief of these defendants. All which matters and things these defendants are ready to aver and prove, as this court shall direct, and pray to be hence dismissed, with their reasonable costs and charges, in this behalf most wrongfully sustained. G. MADDOCKS.

Titles of Answers.

(By an infant.) The answer of C. D., an infant, under the age of twenty-one years, by J. E., his guardian (one of the), defendant, to the bill of complaint of A. B., complainant.

(By a single defendant.) The answer of C. D., defendant, to the bill of complaint of A. B., complainant.

(Joint answer by adults and infants.) The joint and several answers of P. H., and R., his wife, and of D. V. and C. R., infants, under the age of twenty-one years, by G. M. D., their guardian, defendants to the bill of complaint of A. B., complainant.

(Where the bill misstates the names of defendants.) The joint and several answers of J. D., in the bill called W. D., and of C. F., in the bill called G. F., defendants to the bill of complaint of A. B., complainant.

(By husband and wife.) The joint answer of C. D., and S., his wife, defendants, etc.

(By a lunatic or idiot.) The joint answer of C. D., a lunatic (or idiot, or habitual drunkard), by J. T., his guardian *ad litem*, and J. T., committee of the said C. D., defendants to the bill of complaint, etc.

Commencements of Answers.

(Joint answer.) These defendants, and (as in form above) each answering for himself, and not the one for the other, jointly and severally answer, and say that, etc., and these defendants deny all, etc.

(By an infant.) This defendant, answering by his said guardian, saith that he is an infant of the age of —— years, or thereabouts, and he therefore submits his rights and interests in the matters in question in this cause to the protection of this honorable court; without this, that, etc.

(By a formal party, who is a stranger to the facts.) This defendant, saving and reserving to himself, etc. (as in form above), answers and says that he is a stranger to all and singular the matters and things in the said complainant's bill of complaint contained, and, therefore, leaves the complainant to make such proof thereof as he shall be able to produce; without this, that, etc.

Conclusions of Answers.

(Where a party claims the same benefit of defense as if the bill had been demurred to for want of equity.) And this defendant submits to this honorable court that all and every of the matters in the said complainant's bill, mentioned and complained of, are matters which may be tried and determined at law, and with respect to which the said complainant is not entitled to any relief from a court of equity; and this defendant hopes he shall have the same benefit of this defence as if he had demurred to the said complainant's bill. And this defendant denies, etc.

The answer must be signed and sworn to by the defendant, unless the plaintiff, in his bill, should expressly dispense with the necessity of doing so. The answer of a corporation aggregate is put in under their common seal. Where an infant is defendant, his answer is put in by a guardian *ad litem*, appointed specially for that purpose by the court. It is usual for the guardian to file a mere general answer, submitting the rights of the infant to the court; but it is his duty to ascertain the rights of his ward, and to put in a special answer where it is necessary or advisable. And the infant, on becoming of age, is entitled to an order, allowing him to put in a new answer, upon his showing to the satisfaction of the court that it is necessary to protect his rights. A married woman answers with her husband; except when, under special circumstances, and by order of court, she is allowed to answer separately, when she answers by her next friend.

There is still another species of defense to which it is sometimes necessary for a defendant to resort, in conjunction with one or more or all of those which have been already mentioned. Where the defendant is unable to make a complete defense to the plaintiff's bill, without the possession of some facts which rest in the knowledge of the plaintiff himself, or some of the co-defendants to the suit, it may become expedient, for the purpose of procuring such discovery, to exhibit a cross-bill against the plaintiff, or such co-defendant. A cross-bill is not, however, confined to cases in which a discovery is necessary, but is proper whenever a full decree, by which justice is done to all parties, can not be rendered, without giving to two or more defendants an opportunity of litigating some question which arises in a cause. Unless the cross-bill is filed for the purpose of relief as well as discovery, in which case it partakes of the nature of an original bill, it is regarded as a mere auxiliary proceeding, which does not impose upon the plaintiff the necessity of alleging any ground of equity to support the jurisdiction of the court. The cross-bill was derived from the canon law. When the *reus*, or defendant, was brought in to answer, he was said to be convened, which in the language of canonists was called *conventio*, because the plaintiff and defendant met to contest; and since the defendant might have demands against the plaintiff, he had liberty to exhibit a bill against him also, which they called *re conventio*.

Form of a Cross Bill, in the nature of a plea puis darrein continuance.

(Usual commencement.) Complaining showeth unto your honor, your orator, A. B., of, etc., that C. D., of, etc., the defendant hereinafter named, on or about the —— day of ——, filed his bill of complaint in this honorable court against your orator, thereby praying (state the prayer in the bill), and your orator being duly served with process subpœna, appeared and put in his answer thereto, to which answer the said C. D. replied; and issue being thus joined, witnesses were examined on both sides and the proofs closed; whereupon the said cause was noticed for hearing by the said C. D., before your honor as by said bill, and other pleadings and proceeding in the said cause, now remaining filed as of record in this honorable court, reference being thereunto had, will more fully appear.

And your orator further showeth unto your honor that the said cause has not yet been heard; and on or about —— the said C. D., by a certain writing of release bearing date the —— day of ——, did demise, release, and forever quit claim, unto your orator, his heirs, executors, administrators, the several matters and things complained of in and by the said bill of the said C. D., and in question in the said suit, and each and every of them, and of all sums of money then due and owing, or thereafter to become due or owing, together with all, and all manner of actions, causes of actions, suits, and demands whatsoever, both at law and in equity or otherwise howsoever, which he, the said C. D., then had, or which he should or might at any time or times hereafter have, claim, allege, or demand, against your orator, for or by reason or means of any matter, cause, or thing whatsoever, from the beginning of the world to the day of the date of the said deed or writing of release; as by the said release, reference being thereunto had, will appear. And your orator hoped that in consequence of the said release the said C. D. would not have proceeded in the said suit against your orator; but the said C. D., combining and confederating, notwithstanding the said release, threatens and intends to proceed in the said suit, and to bring the said cause on for hearing in due course; and he pretends that no such release was ever executed by him, or if so, that the same was obtained by fraud and surprise, and therefore void. Whereas, your orator charges that the same was in every respect fairly and properly obtained by your orator, and duly executed by the said C. D.

And your orator further charges that under the circumstances aforesaid he is unable to put the said release in issue, or to use the same as a plea in bar in the said suit. All which actings and pretenses are contrary to equity and good conscience, and tend to the injury and oppression of your orator.

In tender consideration whereof, and forasmuch as

your orator has no remedy without the assistance of a court of equity, etc.

To the end, therefore (interrogatories), and that the said release may be established, and declared by this honorable court a sufficient bar to any further proceedings by the said C. D., in the said suit; and that the bill of the said C. D. therein, may, under the circumstances, be forthwith dismissed with costs (and for general relief).

May it please (prayer for subpena).

In the English practice the answer of a defendant who resides in the country, *i. e.*, beyond twenty miles from London, is taken by commissioners appointed for that purpose. The form of the commission is as follows:

A Dedimus Potestatem in Chancery to take a Defendant's Plea, Answer, or Demurrer.

George the Third, by the grace of God, of Great Britain, France, and Ireland, King, Defender of the Faith, and so forth. To Andrew Simpson, Giles Mathew, William Fife, and Peter Sandes, greeting:

Whereas, James Willis has lately exhibited his bill of complaint before us, in our court of chancery, against Edward Willis and William Willis, defendants. And whereas, we have, by our writ, lately commanded the said defendant, Edward Willis, to appear before us in our said chancery, at a certain day now past, to answer the said bill.

Know ye, that we have given unto you, or any three or two of you, full power and authority, "in pursuance of the special order of our said court," to take the answer of the said defendant, Edward Willis, on his corporal oath, upon the holy evangelists; "or his plea upon his corporal oath," to be administered by you, or three or two of you; "or his plea or demurrer without oath," to be respectively made to the said bill; and, therefore, we command you, or any three or two of you, that, at such day and place as you shall think fit, you go to the said defendant, if he can not conveniently come to you, and take his several answer, plea, or demurrer, respectively, as aforesaid, to the said bill, the same being plainly and distinctly written upon parchment; and when you shall have so done, you are to send the same closed up under the seals of you, or any three or two of you, unto us in our said court of chancery, without delay, wheresoever it shall be, together with this writ.

Witness ourself at Westminster, the ——— day of ——— in the thirty-sixth year of our reign.

ARDEN,
WINTER.

Indorsed, " By the court."

If the plaintiff conceives that the admissions of the defendant's answer are alone sufficient to substantiate his case and entitle him to a decree of the court, he may proceed to set down the cause for hearing on bill and answer; but if the discovery is incomplete, or the allegations of the bill insufficiently replied to, the plaintiff may prefer exceptions to the defendant's answer and require it to be more full and particular.

CHAPTER IV.

EXCEPTIONS TO A DEFENDANT'S ANSWER.

If the answer of the defendant, when filed, appears to be defective or evasive, or scandalous and impertinent, the plaintiff may take advantage of such insufficiency by exceptions in writing thereto, in like manner as the defendant may avail himself of objections to the plaintiff's bill by plea or demurrer. The resemblance which generally prevails between the practice of our courts of equity and that of the ancient civil law does not extend to this proceeding. Exceptions to the defendant's answer are purely creatures of our own practice; the *dilationes*, or exceptions of the civil law, being confined to the *libellus articulatus*, or bill, and answering in a great measure to the plea and demurrer of our courts. In truth, the *responsio* of the civil law could hardly admit of exceptions, for there the defendant was examined upon the charges of the *libel viva voce* by the judge, who obliged him, on pain of contumacy, to give direct and unequivocal answers to each article. Such, too, was the early English practice; the masters in chancery, and the barons of the exchequer, being accustomed to take the defendant's answer to the several interrogatories of the bill, from his own mouth. But this duty, when subsequently intrusted to counsel and commissioners, was sometimes so negligently performed as to render the admission of exceptions necessary in justice to the parties. These exceptions must be in writing, and signed by counsel, and they must also state, with precision and accuracy, the points in which the defendant's answer is defective, or they will be rejected as vague and impertinent.

And care must be taken to omit no point to which an exception would lie, as the rules of the court do not permit any others to be afterward added. No exception can be taken to the answer of an infant, because he is not bound by it, and may put in a new answer when he becomes of age. It may be stated generally that any answer will be considered insufficient, in which the defendant does not fully respond, according to the best of his knowledge, remembrance or belief, to every material allegation, charge or interrogatory in the bill. The following is the usual

Form of Exceptions to an Answer in Chancery.

Between { James Willis, by, etc.
Complainant,
and
Edward and Wm. Willis,
Defendants.

Exceptions taken by the said complainant to the joint answer of the said defendants to his bill of complaint in this cause.

First Exception.—For that the said defendants have not, according to the best of their information, knowledge and belief, set forth and discovered in their said answer, whether the said testator, Thomas Atkins, in the complainant's said bill named, duly made and executed such last will and testament in writing, of such date, and of such purport and effect as in said bill mentioned, etc. (pursuing the words of such interrogatories of the bill as are not sufficiently answered.)

Second Exception.—For that the said defendants have not, according to the best of their knowledge, information and belief, set forth and answered whether the said complainant hath or hath not, by his father and next friend, applied to the said defendants, etc., or how otherwise.

In all which particulars the complainant is advised that the answer of the defendants is altogether evasive, imperfect, and insufficient. Wherefore, said complainant doth except thereto, and prays that the defendants may be compelled to amend the same, and to put in a full and sufficient answer to the complainant's bill.

A. MANNING.

If the answer was filed in term time, the plaintiff is allowed eight days after the expiration of the term to file his exceptions; if the answer was filed in vacation, he shall have till the same period in the term immediately following. If exceptions are not filed within these periods, the plaintiff is supposed to acquiesce in the defendant's answer; unless, indeed, upon application to the court, he afterward obtains leave to file them *nunc pro tunc*. If the defendant allows the propriety of the plaintiff's exceptions, he must, within the time limited by the practice of the court, put in a further answer. But if the defendant thinks his answer to be sufficient, the plaintiff may enter an order, which is, of course, to refer the bill, answer, and exceptions taken thereto, to a master, who is directed to report whether the answer is sufficient in the points excepted to or not. If the master reports it to be insufficient, the defendant must submit to answer more particularly, unless, by exceptions to such report of the master, he appeals to the judgment of the court, and obtains a determination in his favor. The following is the form of

Exceptions to a Master's Report as to the Sufficiency of an Answer.

In Chancery. { Between James Willis, by John Willis, his father and next friend, Complainant, and Edward Willis and Wm. Willis, Defendants.

Exceptions taken by the complainant to the report of

E. Leeds, Esq., one of the masters of this court, made in this cause, and bearing date the —— day of —— 1798.

First Exception.—That the said master has stated in his report, That, etc. (pursuing the words of the report), but the said master has not stated, or set forth, etc. (according to the nature of the objections.)

Second Exception.—That, etc.

In all which particulars the complainant doth except to the master's report, and humbly appeals therefrom to this honorable court.   WADMAN.

If the defendant, on the confirmation of the master's report, persists in putting in an evasive or insufficient answer, the court, to punish his contumacy and compel his obedience, may commit him to prison, and direct the bill of the plaintiff to be taken *pro confesso*.

CHAPTER V.

INTERLOCUTORY PROCEEDINGS.

It would be impracticable, in a treatise of this nature, to describe every proceeding which the variety of circumstances occasionally attending the different stages of a suit may by possibility render necessary during its progress. The present seems a fit place to notice the most usual and important, which relate either to amendments of the pleadings, the appointment of a receiver, the payment of money in a court, or references to a master.

These interlocutory applications may be made either orally, by motion, or where they partake of the nature of decretal orders, by petition in writing. A motion can be made only by or on behalf of a party to the record; a petition may be preferred by any person, whether a party to the suit or not. These applications are addressed to the sound discretion of the court, and wherever its special interposition is invoked, must be supported by an affidavit of the party to the facts on which they depend.

1. *Amendment of Pleadings.*

In a court of equity, which looks to the real and substantial merits of a case, matters of form are never suffered to prejudice the rights of a party; and the liberty of amendment, in a greater or less degree, is allowed to all kinds of pleading. Whenever the plaintiff discovers a defect in his bill, arising from want of parties, or other reason, provided the cause is not at issue, he may obtain leave (as of course) to amend his bill. If the defendant, however, has put in his answer, the plaintiff can introduce no matter by way of amendment, which has occurred since the filing of the bill. The amended bill must state so much of the original bill as may be necessary to introduce the amendments and no more. The amended and original bill are considered, for most purposes, as one, and make up the same record; and if the defendant has once appeared, it is unnecessary to serve him with a fresh subpena.

The rule is much more strict as to answers and pleas put in upon oath. The court is exceedingly slow and reluctant in acceding to applications to amend an answer in material facts. Where a defendant has, through inadvertency, mistaken a date, or fallen into any verbal inaccuracy, he will be allowed to correct it; so, where the party relies upon new facts which have come to his knowledge since the answer was put in, or where it is manifest that he is taken by surprise, or where the mistake is a mere oversight, there is less reason to object to the amendment, than where the whole bearing of the facts must have been well known before the answer was put in.

2. *Appointment of a Receiver.*

Wherever there is danger of the waste or destruction of property, which is the subject of litigation, the court may commit it to the custody of a receiver during the pendency of the suit. A receiver may be appointed either before or after answer, or after a decree; but to authorize an application before the hearing, the bill must state facts which show its necessity and propriety, and contain a prayer for the appointment. The court will not, however, appoint a receiver before answer, unless it clearly appears, upon affidavit, that there is danger to the property or fund from the fraud or insolvency of the party having possession of it, or from some other reason.

3. *Payment of Money into Court.*

Whenever it appears, either by the defendant's answer, or upon his examination before a master, or by a master's report, that a balance of money admitted to be due is in his hands, the court will direct it to be paid in. The court will not make this order before answer, unless in a case of manifest fraud. In the case of an executor admitted to have property of the testator in his hands, it was formerly supposed that the plaintiff must show either an abuse of his trust by an executor, or danger to the fund from his insolvency; but an admission of a balance in his hands after payment of debts, is now held to be sufficient to justify the order.

The court will, in its discretion, direct money which has been paid in, either to be deposited for safe-keeping in bank, or to be invested on good security.

4. *The Reference to a Master.*

This is a proceeding of such frequent occurrence and great importance, as to form the subject of a subordinate system of practice. It occurs whenever the court feels an inability to grant relief without some preliminary information. The matters of reference are almost as numerous as the subjects of the jurisdictions of the court. Wherever it is necessary in the progress of a cause to take an account, to investigate the title of persons to property in suit, or make any other inquiries necessary to satisfy the conscience of the chancellor, or to perform some special ministerial act, such as to sell property, settle conveyances, or appoint new trustees, etc., the court refers the matter to a master. And to facilitate the performance of his duties, he is empowered to examine witnesses, and even parties to the cause, by interrogatories. This extra judicial mode of investigation is of very great advantage, not only as the means of relieving the court from burdensome and sometimes inconsistent duties, which are nevertheless necessary to the administration of justice, but as the means of extending the benefit of its jurisdiction to a much greater variety of cases.

Order for Production of Papers before Hearing.

On motion, etc., ordered that the defendant do, within three weeks, leave with the assistant register of this court, the several books of account, accounts, letters, and papers, relating to the matters in this cause, admitted by his answer to be in his possession; and the complainant, his solicitor, agent, or counsel, is to be at liberty to inspect and peruse the same, and to take copies thereof, or extracts therefrom, as he may be advised, at his own expense; but the said defendant is to be at liberty to seal, upon oath, such parts of the said several books, etc., as do not in any manner relate to the matters in controversy in this suit.

Order that Plaintiff Elect—and Election.

It appearing that the complainant prosecutes the defendant both at law and in this court, for one and the same matter, whereby he is doubly vexed, thereupon, on motion of, etc., it is ordered that the complainant, within eight days after notice of this order, elect whether he will proceed at law in the suit brought by him against the defendant, or in this court upon his bill; and if he elects to proceed at law, or if he neglects to file such election within the said eight days, the bill in this cause shall thereupon stand dismissed with costs; and, if he elects to proceed here, it is then further ordered that he proceed no further in the said suit at law without leave of this court.

Order to Pay Money into Court.

On reading and filing bill and answer in this cause, and due proof of service of this motion; and on motion of the plaintiff by his counsel, and after hearing the defendant by his counsel (or, and *no one appearing to oppose the same*), it is ordered that the defendant, C. D., do, on or before the —— day of —— next, pay into the hands of the register of this court, in trust, in this cause, the sum of $——, admitted by the answer of the said defendant to be due from him; and that when such money is paid in, it be deposited by said register, in trust, in the bank of —————— (*or invested in bond and mortgage, in trust*) to the credit of this cause; there to remain until the further order of this court.

Order of Reference to a Master, to appoint a Receiver.

On reading and filing affidavits, and the pleadings in this cause, and on motion of J. E., solicitor for the plaintiff, the defendant being heard by counsel in opposition thereto, ordered that it be referred to a master of this court to appoint a receiver of the rents and profits of the estate, (or of the *estate, property, and effects*) of the defendant, C. D., mentioned in the pleadings in this cause, with the usual powers, and upon the usual directions; and that said master take from such receiver the necessary and usual security for the performance of his trust, and file the same in the proper office; and that upon the filing of the report of the master, and of such security, such receiver be invested with all his rights and powers as receiver, according to the rules and practice of this court.

CHAPTER VI.

OF REPLICATION AND REJOINDER.

If the answer of the defendant controverts the facts charged in the plaintiff's bill, or sets forth new facts and circumstances, which the plaintiff is not disposed to admit (both of which is usually the case), he may maintain the truth of his own allegations, and deny the validity of those alleged by the other party, in a replication to the defendant's answer. This replication, according to the modern practice, consists of a general averment only, of the truth and sufficiency of the plaintiff's bill, and as general a denial of the same properties in the answer of the defendant; but, formerly, if the defendant's answer stated new facts, in opposition to those alleged in the bill, the plaintiff was accustomed to reply by a special statement of other facts, not before charged. This produced a rejoinder by the defendant, asserting the truth and sufficiency of his answer, and alleging the contrary of the plaintiff's replication. A sur-rejoinder frequently followed the rejoinder, and a rebutter the sur-rejoinder, and so on as long as new facts were set forth by one party and denied by the other. But the expense, inconvenience and delay attending these multifarous pleadings on each side, gave rise to an alteration of the practice. Although we have retained the form of a special replication, it has gone completely out of use, and indeed is prohibited by the rules of the Supreme Court of the United States.

The plaintiff, may, however, obtain the benefit which he could have formerly derived from a special replication by amendment of his bill.

A General Replication to a Defendant's Answer.

In Chancery. { Between James Willis, by his father and next friend, plaintiff, and Edward Willis, and William Willis, defendants.

The replication of James Willis, complainant, to the answer of Edward Willis and William Willis, defendants.

This repliant, saving and reserving to himself all and all manner of advantage of exception which may be had and taken to the manifold errors, uncertainties, and insufficiencies of the answer of the said defendants, for replication thereunto, saith, that he doth and will aver, maintain, and prove his said bill to be true, certain, and sufficient in the law, to be answered unto by the said defendants, and that the answer of the said defendants is very uncertain, evasive, and insufficient in the law to be replied unto by this repliant; without that, that any other matter or thing in the said answer contained materially or effectually in the law, to be replied unto, and not herein and hereby well and sufficiently replied unto, confessed, or avoided, traversed, or denied, is true; all which matters and things this repliant is ready to aver, maintain, and prove, as this honorable court shall direct, and humbly prays as in and by his said bill he hath already prayed.

The Special Replication of J. W., Complainant, to the Answer of D. W. and W. W., Defendants.

This repliant, saving and reserving, etc., for replication unto the answer of the said defendant, saith, that he, this repliant, doth, in and by this his replication, waive his demands of tithes of Easter offerings, demanded by his bill, and mentioned in the said defendant's said answer, and does in no wise insist thereupon, or require or intend any examination of witnesses in this cause, concerning or respecting the same, and only insists upon his other demands, made in and by his said bill; and that he doth and will aver, maintain, and prove his said bill, as to all the demands therein contained (except only as to those hereinbefore excepted and waived), to be just and true, certain and sufficient in the law to be answered unto by the said defendant, and that the answer of the said defendant is untrue, uncertain, and insufficient in the law to be replied unto by this repliant, for divers manifest errors and uncertainties therein contained, without that, etc.; all which matters and things this repliant is ready to aver, maintain, and prove, as this honorable court shall direct, and prays in and by his said bill, as he has already prayed, except as hereinbefore excepted.

The plaintiff, having filed his replication, proceeds to serve the defendant with a subpena to rejoin, and to join in commission for the examination of witnesses. The form of this subpena is precisely the same as the common subpena *ad respondendum*, and returnable and served in the same manner. The subpena to rejoin answers to a similar citation in the civil law, which closed the *litis contestatio*, and the reason given by the civilians for its introduction was probably that which occasioned its adoption by our courts of equity, namely, that unless the defendant was cited before the examination of witnesses, the *receptio testium* would be a mere nullity, as the defendant would have no opportunity of inquiring into their credibility, or of cross-examining them. But it is not necessary with them, nor is it with us, that the defendant should appear to the citation, because, as it is a process entirely in his favor, he is left to avail himself of it or not, at his discretion. The cause is therefore completely at issue upon the mere service of the subpena, and no rejoinder is, in general, actually filed. In the United States, generally, if not universally, the pleadings terminate with the replication, and the cause is deemed fully at issue.

The rejoinder (when used) asserts the truth and sufficiency of the defendant's answer, and avers the contrary of the plaintiff's replication in the following form:

A Rejoinder of a Defendant to the Plaintiff's Replication.

The rejoinder of Edward Willis and William Willis, defendants, to the replication of James Willis, an infant complainant.

These defendants, saving and reserving to themselves, severally, all and all manner of benefit and advantage of exception which may be had or taken to the many uncertainties, imperfections, and insufficiencies of and in the replication of the said complainant, for rejoinder to the same, do severally say (in all and every matter and thing as in and by their said answer they have said) they will severally aver, justify, maintain, and prove their said answer in all and every matter, clause, sentence, article, and allegation therein contained, to be just and true, and certain, and sufficient in the law to be replied unto, in such sort, manner and form as in their said answer the same are set forth and declared, and that the said replication is very untrue, uncertain, and insufficient in the law to be rejoined unto by these defendants, without that, that any other matter or thing in the said replication contained, material or effectual in the law to be rejoined unto by these defendants, and not herein and hereby well and sufficiently rejoined unto, confessed or avoided, traversed or denied, is true; all which matters and things these defendants are ready to aver and prove, as this honorable court shall award and direct; and these defendants pray, as in and by their said answer they have already severally prayed.

The cause being now completely at issue, the parties proceed to prove the several allegations contained in their respective pleadings by the examination of witnesses.

CHAPTER VII.

INTERLOCUTORY BILLS.

Several kinds of bills, by which a suit in equity may be commenced, have been noticed in a previous page; but, besides these original bills by which a suit is instituted, there are others of an *auxiliary* nature, by which it may be added to, continued, or revived, as circumstances render necessary. These, arising between the original institution and final determination of a suit, may not improperly be denominated interlocutory bills; and, as they can in no wise become requisite till after issue joined between the parties, prior to which (agreeably to the practice of civil law) any defect in the suit may be remedied by amendment, this seems to be the most proper place for adverting to them. They are:

1. *A Supplemental Bill,*

Which is used for the purpose of supplying some irregularity discovered in the formation of the original bill, or in some of the proceedings upon it; or some defect in the suit, arising from events happening after an issue had been reached in the proceedings, and by which persons not parties to the suit have acquired an interest in it. But the court will not ordinarily permit a supplemental bill to be filed where the defect can be supplied by amendment. This bill, after reciting the original bill and the proceedings which have been had upon it, the circumstances which render the supplemental matter necessary, and the respect in which the state of the cause and the parties is varied by such circumstances, proceeds:

To the end, therefore, that the said E. W. and W. W.

may severally answer all and every the matters and things herein before charged by way of supplement, and that they may discover and set forth, etc. And that your orator may be relieved in the premises as the nature and circumstances of his case may require, may it please your honor to grant subpœna, etc.

If the suit becomes abated by any event subsequent to its institution, it may be renovated by

2. *Bill of Revivor.*

And if the event occasioning the abatement does not affect the interest transmitted in such a manner as to make it subject to litigation in a court of equity, the suit may be continued by bill of revivor *merely*. A familiar illustration occurs in the case of the death of a party whose interest in the subject-matter of the suit is not thereby determined, but transmitted to his personal or real representative, according to the nature of the property upon which the question arises; or upon the marriage of a female plaintiff. The death of one of the parties to a suit, however, does not, in all cases, necessarily produce such an abatement as to suspend all further proceedings, for the persons remaining before the court may have such an interest in the matter in litigation as to be competent to call upon it for a decree. Thus, where several creditors sue on their own behalf, and that of other creditors, the death of one will not abate the proceedings. Where there are several plaintiffs or several defendants, all having an interest which survives, the death of any one of them makes an abatement only as to himself, and the suit is continued as to the rest who are living; unless, indeed, anything is required to be done by or against the interest of the person who is dead.

Form of Bill of Revivor against Heir-at-Law of Deceased Mortgagor.

In Chancery.

Before, etc.   To, etc.

Complaining, shows unto your honor, your orator, J. B., of the city of New York, merchant, that on or about the —— day of —— last past, your orator filed his bill in this honorable court against L. M., since deceased, and others, stating therein the due execution and acknowledgments by the said L. M. of a certain indenture of mortgage, dated the —— day of —— in the year 1829, for securing the payment to your orator of the sum of $3,000, lawful money of the United States, according to the condition of a certain bond or obligation therein mentioned, and which indenture of mortgage comprised a house and lot of ground, lying in the —— ward of the city of New York; and further stating that the said L. M. had made default in the payment of the said sum of money, according to the condition of such bond, and thereupon praying (set out the prayer of the bill) as by such bill on file in this court will on reference appear.

And your orator further shows that the said L. M., being duly served with process, appeared to the said original bill, and put in his answer thereto; and the said cause being at issue, the same came on to be heard on the ——, when the court was pleased to order and decree, etc.

And your orator further shows unto your honor that some proceedings have been had before the master to whom this cause stands referred; but no report hath yet been made thereon. And, further, that on or about the ——, the said late defendant, L. M., departed this life, leaving B. D., of —— (the defendant hereinafter named), his heir-at-law, and without having devised, or in any manner disposed of, the equity of redemption of and in the said mortgaged premises.

And your orator further shows unto your honor, that the said suit having become abated by the death of the said late defendant, your orator is, as he has been advised, entitled to have the said suit revived against the said B. D., as the heir at law of the said L. M., and to have the said decree and other proceedings had thereon prosecuted and carried into full effect against the said B. D., in like manner as they could or might have had if the said late defendant had been still living. To the end, therefore, that the said B. D. may show cause, if he can, why the said suit and proceedings therein should not stand and be revived against him as such heir at law of the said late defendant as aforesaid, and be in the same plight and condition as the same were in at the time of the abatement thereof; and that the said suit and proceedings had therein, may stand and be revived accordingly; may it please your honor to grant unto your orator the writ of subpena to revive the same, issuing out of and under the seal of this honorable court, to be directed to the said B. D., thereby commanding him, by a certain day, and under a certain penalty, to be therein expressed, personally to be and appear before your honor, in this honorable court, and then and there to show cause, if he can, why the said suit, and the proceedings therein had, should not stand and be revived against him, and be in the same plight and condition as the same were at the abatement thereof; and further, to stand to and abide such order and decree in the premises as to your honor may seem meet.

And your orator will ever pray, etc.

If, however, the event which occasions the abatement be accompanied with other circumstances necessary to be stated to the court, in order to obtain a complete decree, such circumstances must be stated by way of supplemental bill, added to the bill of revivor.

But if the abatement of the suit happen by an event

which may occasion the interest transmitted to be contested, the benefit of the suit can not be obtained by a bill of revivor, *eo nomine*, but must be sought by

3. *An Original Bill, in the nature of a Bill of Revivor.*

It is said to be original, merely for want of a privity of title between the parties to the former, and those to the latter suit, and when the validity of the alleged transmission of interest is established, the suit is in the same situation as it would have been by bill of revivor merely, in case the establishment of such interest had been unnecessary. This bill, like the bill of revivor, states the original bill and proceedings, the abatement, and the manner in which the interest of the party deceased has been transmitted; and it must likewise charge the validity of such transmission, and state the facts which have accrued under it.

If, again, the interest of a party to the suit be, by any event, wholly determined, and the property become vested in others not claiming under him, the benefit of the original suit can not be obtained by either of the last mentioned bills, but by

4. *An Original Bill, in the nature of a Supplemental Bill.*

This bill must state the original bill, and the proceedings had under it; the event which caused the abatement of the suit; and the manner in which the property in dispute has become vested in the persons entitled; show the equitable grounds upon which the parties are entitled to the benefit of the former suit; and pray a decree of the court adapted to the nature of the plaintiff's case.

A bill for this purpose seems to differ from an original bill in the nature of a bill of revivor, in this, that upon an original bill, in the nature of a bill of revivor, the benefit of the former proceeding is absolutely obtained; so that the pleadings in the first cause, as also the depositions of witnesses (if any have been taken), may be used in the same manner as if they had been filed or taken in the second cause; and if any decree has been made in the first cause, the same decree will be made in the second cause. But in the case of an original bill, in the nature of a supplemental bill, a new defense may be made; the pleadings and depositions can not be used to the same extent as if filed or taken in the same cause; and the decree, if any has been obtained, is no otherwise of advantage than as it may be an inducement to the court to make a similar decree.

CHAPTER VIII.

OF EXAMINATION OF WITNESSES.[1]

In the several proceedings which we have hitherto had occasion to enumerate, as applicable to our courts of equity, the reader has perceived a great resemblance in *substance*, though generally a difference in *form*, to those used in our courts of common law. But in the examination of witnesses, a material difference prevails, both in form and effect. The examinations in courts of law being *ore tenus*, in the presence of the judge and the court; and impromptu at the time of trial; whilst that in the courts of equity, agreeably to the civil law, is conducted in *private*, and upon interrogatories or questions in writing previously framed for the purpose.

If the witnesses reside within twenty miles of London, this examination is taken before a public officer appointed by the court for that particular purpose; but if they reside beyond that distance, a commission or *dedimus potestatem* is granted to four commissioners (two nominated by each party) authorizing them to take the depositions of the several witnesses at the respective places of their residence.

---

[1] The English practice in relation to the examination of witnesses and the preparations of causes for hearing has been greatly modified in all of the United States. The student must look to the local statutes.

A Commission to examine Witnesses in Chancery.

George the Third, by the grace of God, of Great Britain, France, and Ireland, King, Defender of the Faith, and so forth, to Samuel Johnson, Mayat Edwards, William Mason, and Peter Warne, greeting:

Know ye, that we, in confidence of your prudence and fidelity, have appointed you, and by these presents do give unto you, any three or two of you, full power and authority diligently to examine all witnesses whatsoever upon certain interrogatories to be exhibited to you, as well on the part of James Willis, complainant, as on the part of Edward Willis and William Willis, defendants, or either of them; and therefore we command you, any three or two of you, that at certain days and places, to be appointed by you for that purpose, you do cause the said witnesses to come before you, and then and there examine each of them apart, upon the said interrogatories, on their respective corporal oaths, first taken before you, any three or two of you, upon the holy evangelists; and that you do take such their examinations, and reduce them into writing on parchment; and when you shall have so taken them, you are to send the same to us in our chancery, without delay, wheresoever it shall then be, closed up and under your seals, or the seals of three or two of you, distinctly and plainly set forth, together with the said interrogatories, and this writ: And we further command you and every of you, that before you act in, or be present at the swearing or examining any witness or witnesses, you do severally take the oath first specified in the schedule hereunto annexed; and we do give you, any three, two, or one of you, full power and authority, jointly or severally, to administer such oath to the rest or any other of you, upon the holy evangelists; and we further command that all and every the clerk or clerks employed in taking, writing, transcribing, or ingrossing the deposition or depositions of witnesses to be examined by virtue of these presents, shall, before he or they be permitted to act as clerk or clerks as aforesaid, or be present at such examination, severally take the oath last specified in the said schedule annexed; and we also give you, or any of you, full power and authority, jointly and severally, to administer such oath to such clerk or clerks, upon the holy evangelists.

Witness ourself at Westminster, the —— day of ——, in the 36th year of our reign.   ARDEN,
                 WINTER.

Indorsed, "By order of court."

Label.—To Samuel Johnson, Mayat Edwards, William Mason, and Peter Warne, Gentlemen, any three or two of them to examine witnesses, as well on the part of James Willis, plaintiff, as on the part of Edward Willis and William Willis, defendants, returnable without delay, on fourteen days' notice to the defendants.

                  ARDEN,
                  WINTER.

Proper notice having been given to the defendants of the time and place of executing the commission, interrogatories or questions, previously framed and settled, are produced on each side, and separately read to the respective witnesses, and their responses or depositions taken down in writing by the commissioners. Interrogatories should be concise and to the point, not leading or directing. The following is the usual form:

Interrogatories exhibited in Equity.

Interrogatories to be administered to witnesses to be produced, sworn, and examined in a certain cause depending in the high court of chancery, wherein James Willis, by John Willis, his father and next friend, is complainant, and Edward Willis and William Willis, executors of the last will and testament of Thomas Atkins, deceased, are defendants. On the part and behalf of the said complainant; that is to say—

First interrogatory.—Do you know the parties, complainants and defendants, in the title of these interrogatories named, or any and which of them, and how long, etc., etc.? Declare the truth and your knowledge therein.

Second interrogatory.—Did or did not the said Thomas Atkins, in the foregoing interrogatories named, ever, and when and where, in your sight or presence, or in the presence of any and what other person or persons, to your knowledge, sign, seal, publish, or declare, his last will and testament, in writing, or any other and what writing, as for or purporting to be, his last will, etc., etc.? Declare, etc.

Third interrogatory.—Do you know of any application or applications which have been made by or on the behalf of the above named complainant, to the defendants above named, or either and which of them, for the payment of the legacy of £800, in the pleadings in this cause mentioned to have been bequeathed to or for the benefit of the said complainant, etc. If yea, set forth when, or about what time or times respectively, and by whom, by name, and to whom, and where such application or applications was or were so made, and whether the same was or were, in any and what manner, complied with or assented to, or refused and rejected, and by whom, and for any and what reasons? Declare, etc.

Lastly.—Do you know of any other matter or thing, or have you heard, or can you say, anything touching the matters in question in this cause, that may tend to the benefit and advantage of the complainant in this cause, besides what you have been interrogated unto? If yea, declare the same fully, and at large, as if you had been particularly interrogated thereto.

A. Manning.

After the oaths have been duly administered to the commissioners, their clerks, and the respective witnesses, the depositions are taken and transcribed in the following form:

Depositions in Equity by Commission.

Depositions of witnesses, produced, sworn, and examined, on the —— day of ——, in the thirty-sixth year of his present Majesty, King George the Third, and in the year of our Lord 1795, at the house of W. Brown, known by the sign of the Bush, situated in the parish of Kelsal, in the county of Nottingham, by virtue of a commission issuing out of his Majesty's high court of chancery, to us, Samuel Johnson, William Mason, and others, directed, for the examination of witnesses in a cause therein depending, between James Willis, by John Willis, his father and next friend, plaintiff, and Edward Willis and William Willis, defendants, on the part and behalf of the said complainant, we, the acting commissioners, under the said commission, and also the respective clerks, by us employed, in taking, writing, transcribing, and engrossing, the said depositions, having first duly taken the oaths annexed to the said commission, according to the tenor and effect thereof, and as thereby required.

James Henry Nevil, of Pelligate, in the county of Northampton, Esq., aged thirty years, or thereabouts, a witness produced, sworn, and examined, on the part and behalf of the said complainant, James Willis, deposeth and saith, as follows:

To the first interrogatory.—This deponent saith, that he knows the said complainant, James Willis, and hath so known him for the space of three years, last past, or thereabouts, and doth also know, and is well acquainted with the said defendants, Edward Willis and William Willis, etc.

To the second interrogatory.—This deponent saith,

that he was present, and did see Thomas Atkins, in the pleadings in this cause mentioned, sign, seal, publish, and declare, as and for his last will and testament, a certain writing, etc., etc.

To the third interrogatory.—This deponent saith that in or about the month of January last, he, this deponent, was, together with John Willis, the father of the said complainant, James Willis, at the house of, and in company with, the said William Willis, and doth well remember that the said John Willis did then and there address the said defendant, on the part and in behalf of the said complainant, and requested that the said William Willis, or his co-executor, the said Edward Willis, would pay or otherwise secure, for the benefit of the said complainant, the said legacy of £800, etc., etc.

And to the last interrogatory.—This deponent saith, he doth not know of any matter or thing, etc., etc.

JAMES HENRY NEVIL,
SAMUEL JOHNSON,
WILLIAM MASON.

If the witness be examined, in town, before the examiner, the form will necessarily vary.

Depositions in Equity, before an Examiner.

Witnesses examined in a cause depending and at issue in this honorable court, wherein James Willis, an infant, by John Willis, his father and next friend, is complainant; and Edward Willis and William Willis are defendants, on the part and behalf of the said complainant, by Alexander Morgan, Esq., examiner in chancery.

James Henry Nevil, of, etc., aged thirty years and upward, being produced as a witness, on the part and behalf of the complainant in this cause, was, on the —— day of ——, in the year of our Lord 1795, shown in person, at the seat of Mr. Hill (who is the clerk in court of the defendants, in the title hereof named), by Mr. Vaugn, one of the sworn clerks in my office, who then also left a note of the name, title, and place of abode of the deponent, at the seat aforesaid; and afterward, on the same day and year, the said deponent, being sworn and examined, deposeth and saith as follows:

1st. —— to the first interrogatories —— the said deponent saith, that, etc. (as before).

A. Morgan,
R. Hinde.

The depositions, being completed, are closely bound up, and (being secured from inspection by the signature and seals of the several commissioners) sent to the court, out of which the commission issued, by a messenger who makes oath "that the said depositions have not been opened or altered since they were delivered to his charge." They are then committed to the custody of the clerk, in court, who prepared the commission, if taken in the county, or detained by the examiner, if taken in town, till publication has passed[1] by rule or order of court. After which they may be inspected, or copies of them delivered, at the request of any of the parties.

After publication has passed the parties regularly are to proceed to a hearing; but should the evidence on either side appear to be exceptionable, on account of the discredit or the incompetency of any of the witnesses, leave may be obtained on motion to object to the validity

---

[1] When the examination of witnesses on both sides is ended, either party serves the other with a rule or order of court, importing that the depositions will be made public, unless sufficient cause be shown against it, within a time therein expressed. If no cause is shown, the rule is made absolute. This is termed "passing publication," and absolves the commissioners and examiner from their respective oaths of secrecy.

of their testimony.¹ The method of doing this is by exhibition of articles in the following form:

Articles of Exception to the Credit of a Witness in Chancery.

Articles exhibited by James Willis, complainant, by John Willis, his father and next friend, in a certain cause now depending and at issue in the high court of chancery, wherein the said James Willis, by his said father, is complainant, and Edward Willis and William Willis are defendants, to discredit the testimony of Henry James Nevil, a witness examined before Alexander Morgan, Esq., one of the examiners of the said court (or, if the witnesses were examined by commissioners), "by virtue of a commission issued out of the said court, to Samuel Johnson and others, directed for the examination of witnesses in the said cause, upon certain interrogatories exhibited before them for that purpose; and which said witness was examined on the part and behalf of the said defendant.

First. The said James Willis, by his said father and next friend, doth charge and allege that the said Henry James Nevil hath, since his examination in the said cause, acknowledged that he is to receive, and doth expect a considerable reward or gratuity in money, from the said defendant, in case the said cause be determined in his, the said defendant's, favor; and that he, the said Henry James Nevil, is personally interested in the issue or determination of said cause.

Secondly. That said James Willis doth, as aforesaid, charge and allege, that the said Henry James Nevil is a

---

¹ In strictness the proper time and manner of exhibiting objections to the competency of witnesses is by interrogatories at the examination in chief, before the commissioners or examiner; but as their competency is seldom known until after the publication of their depositions, this indulgence is never refused, when grounded upon an affidavit substantiating its propriety.

person of bad morals, and of evil fame and character, and is generally esteemed and reputed so to be; and that the said witness is a person who hath no regard to the sacredness of an oath, or belief in a future state, and one whose testimony is in no respect to be credited.

H. MANNING.

These articles are filed in the office of the examiner, or of the six clerks of the court, accordingly as the original depositions were taken before him, or by commissioners, and interrogatories (by leave of the court) are framed upon them, and exhibited before the examiner in chancery, or by commission, and the depositions taken and published, as in other cases. Exceptions may also be taken to them. These matters being at length finally settled, the parties proceed to a hearing.

CHAPTER IX.

OF THE HEARING OF A CAUSE IN EQUITY.

The cause being now ripe for hearing, it may be set down at the instance of either party, and a subpena to hear judgment procured and served as in other cases.

This subpena corresponds with the notion of the civilians, that no act of court should be made *altera parte inaudita*: and by the ancient rule of the court, there was always a term between passing publication and hearing the cause, that the several suitors might have time to prepare themselves for attendance. See *For. Rom.* 134, 151. But now the rule in chancery is, that the plaintiff shall have liberty to set down his cause for hearing on the next term after publication, and, on failure, it may be set down by the defendant on the term next following; and if the plaintiff do not then appear, his bill will be dismissed for want of prosecution.

The form of this subpena, in chancery, is the same as that we have already given, with a difference only in the label and indorsement, which express the purpose for which the party's attendance is required, as,

Subpena to hear Judgment in Chancery.

George the Third, etc.—To Edward Willis and William Willis, greeting:

For certain causes offered before us in our chancery, we command, etc., that you personally be and appear before us in our said chancery, on the 8th day of November next, wheresoever it shall then be, to answer, etc., (as in the *subpena ad respondendum*). Witness, etc.

Courtenay.

Indorsed.—" By the court, to hear judgment, the 11th

day of November, at the suit of William Willis, an infant."

Label.—Edward Willis to appear in chancery, returnable the 8th day of November next, to hear judgment the 11th day of the same month, at the suit of James Willis, an infant.

The subpena to hear judgment, by the practice of the court, is made returnable three judicial days before that in which the cause is appointed to be heard. These are called days of *grace*, and the reason assigned by Sir William Blackstone for their introduction is, "that our sturdy ancestors held it beneath the condition of freemen to appear or to do any other act at the precise time appointed." The feudal law, therefore, (from whence is derived the *quarto die post* of our common law), as well as the canon and civil law, allowed three distinct days of citation before the defendant was adjudged contumacious for not appearing.

If, however, the defendant be a body corporate, a writ of distringas, instead of the subpena, is to be served upon them, conformably to the practice in requiring their appearance to the bill.

The parties appearing, by their counsel, on the third day after the return of the subpena, the allegations of the plaintiff, and the defendant's answer, are briefly stated to the court, by the junior counsel on each side. The leading counsel of the plaintiff then enters more particularly into the nature, circumstances, and merits of his case, and informs the court of the points in issue between the parties. Such parts of the depositions and answer of the defendant as the plaintiff chooses to call for are then read for the purpose of receiving the remarks and animadversions of his counsel. The defendant afterward proceeds in the same manner to make his defense, and the plaintiff's counsel are heard in reply; which ends the *forensis litigatio;* and the court proceeds to pronounce its decree, which is the final judgment or sentence of the court upon the rights of the several parties in the cause, and is minuted down by the register, from the mouth of the chancellor. But if the defendant neglect to appear by his counsel at the hearing, the counsel for the plaintiff, on proving service of the *subpena ad audiendum judicium*, prays such decree as he deems his client entitled to;[1] which (not being opposed), is granted as of course, with this reservation only, that the defendant, within a given time, shall be at liberty to show cause against its being carried into execution. For this purpose the plaintiff procures a subpena to show cause, which, in chancery is as follows:

A Subpena to show Cause, in Chancery.

George the Third, etc. To Edward Willis, greeting:

For certain causes offered before us, in our chancery, we command and strictly enjoin you, that, laying all other matters aside, and notwithstanding any excuse, you personally be and appear before us, in our said chancery, on the —— day of —— next; wheresoever it shall then be, then and there to show good and sufficient cause, in a certain matter in our said chancery, now in controversy between James Willis, an infant, complainant, and Edward Willis and William Willis, defendants, according to the true intent and meaning of a certain

---

[1] But if, on the other hand, the plaintiff, after setting down his cause for hearing, neglect to attend, the court can only order it to be struck out of the paper of causes to be set down afresh, unless the defendant has taken the precaution to make an affidavit of his having been served with a subpena to hear judgment, at the plaintiff's suit; in which case the bill will be dismissed with costs, "because a plaintiff may set down his cause, and yet, upon further consideration of the matter he may not think fit to serve the defendant with a subpena to hear judgment, in which case it must be heard *ad requisitionem defendentis*, in order to entitle him to a dismission." For. Rom. 157.

order of our said court, made between, etc., in this cause, bearing date the —— day of —— last, and to do further, and receive, etc. (as in the subpena to appear and answer) witness, etc. COURTENAY.

Indorsed, "By the court."

Label.—Edward Willis, to appear in chancery, returnable the —— day of ——, to show cause against a decree dated the —— day of ——, at the suit of James Willis, an infant. COURTENAY.

This subpena is served in the same manner as those which have been formerly described; but there is no rule limited in respect of the time of service, which may therefore be on any day before the return. If the defendant show no cause within the time specified within the order and subpena, or allowed by the indulgence of the court, he is presumed to submit to the requisitions of the decree, and the cause is at an end; but if at the return of the subpena, he offers to the court sufficient reasons against the affirmance of the decree, the cause is restored, and a decree pronounced after a full discussion of the merits of the case.

CHAPTER X.

OF A DECREE IN EQUITY.

A DECREE is the sentence or judgment of the court pronounced after the hearing or submission of the cause. It may be interlocutory or final. The former is properly an order or decree pronounced for the purpose of ascertaining matter of fact or law, preparatory to a final decree. It very seldom happens that the first decree can be final or conclude the cause. The most usual ground for not making a perfect decree in the first instance is the necessity which frequently exists to ascertain a disputed fact, by an issue at law, or to refer a cause to a master of the court, to make inquiries, or to take accounts, or to adjust other matters which must be disposed of before a final decision can be made of the subject-matter of the suit. In England, it is very common, where any difficult question of law is raised, for the chancellor to send a case in which it is presented to one of the common law courts for an opinion; but this practice has never prevailed in the United States. The occasion and manner of referring a cause to a master has been considered in a previous chapter; and it remains for us to explain the anomalous proceeding called a feigned issue, which seems to have been borrowed from the *sponsio judicialis* of the Roman law. If the court, in consequence of the defects incident to all written testimony, is embarrassed in the solution of a question of fact, it may either order a regular action at law, or may direct a master to frame an issue involving the question between the parties, and then require them to proceed at law, as for a wager; the plaintiff in equity being ordinarily the plaintiff at law, and averring in his declaration that a wager has been laid on the truth of the statement in the issue, and the defendant admitting the fact. As this proceeding takes place for the purpose of informing the conscience of the court, it is not strictly bound down to the form and incidents of an ordinary trial. Sometimes it insists on more than the common law tribunal would have been satisfied with; as on the issue *devisavit vel non*, where the examination of all the three witnesses to the will is indispensable; sometimes it is satisfied with less, and directs the examination of the parties themselves, and also the reading of the depositions which may have been previously taken. When the verdict is returned, it having been obtained for the satisfaction of the conscience of the chancellor, he may, if he thinks proper, inquire into all which passed at the trial, and if he is not, under the circumstances, convinced by the verdict, treat it as a nullity.

A decree is final when it fully decides and disposes of the whole merits of the cause, and reserves no further questions or directions for the future judgment of the court. It is not final because it settles one or more material questions involved in a case, if others remain to be determined. So it may be final, although it contains a reference to a master, if it at the same time provides for all the contingencies which may arise upon his report, and leaves no necessity, upon its confirmation, for any further order of the court, to give to all parties the entire benefit of the decision. Of this nature is a decree directing land to be sold, and appointing a commissioner to perform the order and execute a conveyance; a decree ascertaining the amount due, directing a sale, and giving costs; or any decretal order upon which an execution may be taken out.

There are, however, some decrees which, although final in their nature, require the confirmation of a further order of the court, before they can be acted upon. Of this nature are decrees in suits against infants, in which a day is given to the infant to show cause against it, after he attains twenty-one. This is because an infant is always under the protection of the court, and there may be neglect or collusion on the part of his guardian, through whom he answers. Such collusion or fraud, therefore, is the chief ground for reversing a decree after he is of age; or he may show error, or make a new case not before insisted upon. He is not, however, under the necessity of waiting until he becomes of age, to seek redress, but may impeach the decree at any time before it is made absolute, by an original bill.

To the same class belong decrees *nisi*, or by default, which, as we have seen, are incomplete until confirmed and made absolute by a subsequent order of the court. They differ very little in point of form from ordinary decrees, made upon hearing all parties. A decree of this nature is not considered as the judgment of the court, but as the act of the party who obtain it, conceiving what the judgment of the court would be if the other party appeared. And it is taken at his peril, if not supported by the pleadings and proofs.

Where, however, the bill is to be taken *pro confesso*, the proper course seems to be for the court itself to examine the pleadings and pronounce the decree, and not permit the complainant (as in the case of default at the hearing) to take such decree as he thinks will stand.

The court being at length, by certificate of the judges, the verdict of a jury, or the report of a master, possessed of every information necessary to enable it to adjust and decide the rights of all parties, the cause is again brought to hearing, on the equitable matters reserved, and a definite decree rendered, according to equity and good conscience.[1]

---

[1] As we have noticed in a former page the accustomed form of proceeding by the parties at the hearing of a cause in equity, it may

Form of Decrees.

Decrees in general consist of three parts: 1. The date and title. 2. The recitals; and, 3. The ordering part, to which may sometimes be added 4. The declaratory part, which when made use of, generally precedes the ordering part. The decree commences with the name of the court, and the place where it is held, the term at which it is pronounced, and the title of the cause. The practice in England, at one time, was to recite at length the pleadings and evidence in the cause; but this practice, in consequence of its expense and inconvenience, has been abolished, and the decree now merely recites the substance of the pleadings and the facts on which the court founds its judgment. In the United States the decree usually contains a mere reference to the antecedent pleadings, without embodying them, or any special facts upon which it is rendered. After the recitals comes the ordering or mandatory part of the decree, containing the specific directions of the court upon the matter before it, which it is obvious must depend upon the nature of the particular case which is its subject. Where the

---

not be amiss to continue that deduction by subjoining here a short account of the manner in which the decree of the court is taken and recorded. This is done by the register of the court, who minutes down in a book kept for that purpose a memorandum of the person or persons then presiding on the bench and present at the hearing; the names of the counsel on both sides; the evidence and documents read; the objections (if any) made to such evidence; the manner in which such objections were disposed of; and lastly, the final sentence, judgment, or decree of the court, pronounced on the rights and interests of the several parties in the cause. And upon the minutes thus taken, the decree of the court, as afterward drawn up and recorded, is founded; and with which it must in substance exactly correspond; for no part of the decree but what is warranted by the minutes will be binding upon the parties. If, however, they are erroneous, they will be rectified on proper application to the court.

suit seeks a declaration of the rights of the parties, the ordering part of the decree should be prefaced by such declaration. This is not, however, absolutely necessary, and its omission will not invalidate the decree. It may be observed in this place that when a decree is made by consent, it should be so stated. For the better understanding of the subject, the following forms of decrees, in familiar cases, are inserted:

General Form.[1]

Monday, the 12th day of November, 1795, in the thirty-sixth year of the reign of his Majesty, King George the Third; between James Willis, an infant, by John Willis, his father and next friend, plaintiff, and Edward Willis, William Willis, and Samuel Dickenson, defendants.

This cause coming on this day, to be heard and debated before the right honorable the Lord High Chancellor of Great Britain, in the presence of counsel learned on both sides, the substance of the plaintiff's bill appeared to be, that, etc. (here the plaintiff's bill is shortly recited). Therefore that the said defendant may pay, etc. (the prayer of the bill), and to be relieved, is the scope of the plaintiff's bill; whereto the counsel for the

---

[1] The following form of a decree *pro confesso*, is taken from Wilcox's Ohio Forms. It is not the common practice in Ohio to express in a decree the facts upon which the decision of the chancellor is founded.

A. B.
vs. } *In Chancery.*
C. D.

This cause came on to be heard upon the bill, exhibits, and testimony, and the defendant still failing to appear and plead, answer or demur to said bill, the court, on consideration of the premises, do order and decree that the said bill be taken for confessed, and that the said C. D. shall within —— days (the *specific* decree, according to the nature of the case).

defendant alleged that he by answer admits, etc. (the substance of the answer stated); whereupon, and upon debate of the matter, and hearing the will of the said Thomas Atkins, the answers of defendants, etc., and the proofs taken in this cause read, and what was alleged by the counsel on both sides, his lordship declared, that, etc. (the decree of the court).

THURLOW, C.

WINTER, for the plaintiff.

Decree by Default.

(*Title of cause.*) This cause, coming before the court, in the presence of counsel learned for the plaintiff, none appearing for the defendant, although he has been duly served with a subpena, to hear judgment, as by affiant now read, appears: the substance of the plaintiff's bill appearing to be, etc., Whereupon, and upon hearing the defendant's answer read and what was alleged, etc., this court doth think fit, and so order and decree that, etc. And this decree is to be binding upon the defendant, unless he, upon being served with a subpena for that purpose, shall, at the return thereof, show unto this court good cause to the contrary. But the said defendant, before he is to be admitted to show such cause, is to pay unto the plaintiff his costs of this day's default in appearance. To be taxed, etc.

Decree for an Account.

The court doth order and decree that this order be referred to E. H., one of the masters of this court, to take a mutual account of all dealings and transactions between the plaintiff and the defendant, for the better caring of which account, the parties are to produce before the said master, upon oath, all deeds or books, papers and writing in their custody or power, relating thereto, and are to be examined upon interrogatories, as the said master shall direct, who, in taking the said account, is to make unto the parties all just allowances, and to report to the court what upon the balance of said account shall appear to be due from either party to the other. And the court doth reserve the consideration of the costs of this suit, and of all further directions, until after the master shall have made his report, when either side is to be at liberty to apply to the court, as occasion may require.

Decree for a Specific Performance.

(After the usual introduction, proceed). And it appearing to the court that a good title can be made by the complainant to the premises described in the agreement between the parties in this suit, and referred to in the pleadings therein, and it appearing, also, that the said agreement ought to be carried into execution according to the true intent and meaning of the parties thereto, the court doth order and decree that the said agreement, which has been duly proven to have been made and entered into between the complainant and defendant in this suit, be specifically performed. And the court doth further order and decree that the said complainant, G. W., execute and deliver the defendant, H. J., a good and sufficient conveyance in fee of the premises which formed the subject of contract between them, and which are particularly described in their agreement filed among the papers in this cause; and the form of such conveyance is to be settled by E. H., one of the masters of the court, if the parties differ about the same. And the court doth further order and decree that the said defendant, H. J., upon the tender or delivery to him of such conveyance, do pay unto the complainant, G. W., the sum of $——, the balance of the purchase-money of such premises, reported by the master to be still due, with interest thereon at the rate of six per cent. from the date of said report. And the court doth not think fit to give any costs on either side.

Decree in Creditor's Suit.

This court doth order and decree that it be referred to E. H., one, etc., to take an account of what is due to the plaintiffs and all the other creditors of James Robinson, deceased, the intestate in the pleadings mentioned, and of his funeral expenses and such other claims and charges as by law are entitled to a preference in the distribution of the assets of said intestate, and to compute interest on such of the debts as carry interest; and the said master is to cause an advertisement to be published in such of the public papers as he may think fit of the town of ———, for the creditors of the said intestate to come in before him at a place in such advertisement to be named and prove their debts, and he is to fix a peremptory day for that purpose, and in default of their coming in to prove their debts by the time so appointed, they are to be excluded from the benefit of this decree; but the persons so coming in to prove their debts, not parties to this suit, are, before they are to be admitted as creditors, to contribute to the plaintiffs their portion of the expenses of this suit to be settled by the master. And it is ordered that the master do take an account of the personal estate of the said intestate, come to the hands of the said defendant, his administrator, or to the hands of any other person by his order or for his use. And it is ordered that the said intestate's personal estate be applied in payment of his debts and funeral expenses, in due course of administration. And for the better taking of the said accounts, etc. (as ———). And this court doth reserve the consideration of all further directions, and the costs of this suit until, etc. (as ———.)

Decree of Interpleader.

(Usual introduction). This court doth order that the parties do interplead; and for that purpose, the defendants, T. W. and H. W., are ordered to proceed in the action of trover, which they have brought against the plaintiffs, with liberty for the defendants, J. H. and S. M., to defend such action. And this court doth reserve the consideration of the costs of this suit and all further directions until after the trial of said action. And any of the parties are to be at liberty to apply, etc.

Decree of Sale, on Foreclosure of Mortgage.

This cause having been this day brought in to be heard upon the bill of complaint filed therein, taken as confessed by —— ——, and upon the report of —— ——, one of the masters of this court, which report bears date on the —— day of ——, and was made in pursuance of an order of this court, heretofore made in this cause, referring it to him to compute the amount due to the complainant on the bond and mortgage mentioned and set forth in said bill of complaint. On reading and filing said report, from which it appears that there was due to the said complainant at the date of the report, for the said principal and interest, the sum of —— ——, —— and on reading and filing the —— ——, showing the regularity of the proceedings to take the bill in this cause as confessed, and on motion of —— ——, of counsel for the complainant, it is ordered, adjudged and decreed, and this court by virtue of the authority therein vested doth order, adjudge and decree that the said report and all things therein contained do stand ratified and confirmed. And it is further ordered, adjudged and decreed that all and singular the said mortgaged premises mentioned in the bill of complaint in this cause and hereinafter described, or so much thereof as may be sufficient to raise the amount due to the complainant for the principal, interest and costs in this case, and which may be sold separately without material injury to the parties interested, be sold at public auction by or under the direction of one of the masters of this court; that the said sale be made in the county where the said mortgaged premises or the greater part thereof are situated; that the master give public notice of the time and place of such sale, according to the course and practice of this court; and that the complainant or any of the parties in this cause may become the purchaser; that the master execute a deed to the purchaser of the mortgaged premises on the said sale; and that the said master pay to the complainant or solicitor, out of the proceeds of the said sale, costs in this suit to be taxed, and also the amount so reported due as aforesaid, together with legal interest thereon from date of the said report, or so much as the purchase money of the mortgaged premises will pay of the same; and that the master take his receipt for the amount so paid, and file the same with his report; and that he bring the surplus moneys arising from the said sale, if any there be, into court, without delay, to abide the further order of the same. And it is further ordered and adjudged and decreed, that the defendant, and all persons claiming, or to claim, from or under —— be forever barred and foreclosed, of and from all equity of redemption, and claim of, in, and to, the said mortgaged premises, and every part and parcel thereof. And it is further ordered and decreed, that the purchaser or purchasers of the said premises, at such sale be let into the possession of the said premises, or any part thereof; and any person who, since the commencement of this suit, has come in possession under them, or either of them, deliver possession thereof to such purchaser or purchasers, on production of the master's deed for said premises, and a certified copy of the order confirming the report of the sale, after such order had become absolute.[1]

---

[1] The above form is taken from 3 Hoffman's Chancery Practice, 244.

The decree being drawn up and approved, and signed in chancery by the chancellor, it is engrossed on rolls of parchment and deposited amongst the records of the court as a perpetual evidence of the proceedings. If, however, either party thinks himself aggrieved by the decree, he may, before its enrollment, petition the court for a re-hearing. Six months are allowed to the party gaining the cause to enroll the decree; if he delay it till after that time, he must apply to the court to enroll it *nunc pro tunc*, which is granted of course.[2]

---

[2] The enrollment of decrees is now very rare in England; and seems to be in all cases unnecessary. In the United States all decrees in equity, as well as judgment at law, are matters of record, and are deemed to be enrolled, as of the term of the court at which they are declared, whether they are so in fact or not.

CHAPTER XI.

OF RE-HEARING A CAUSE IN EQUITY.[1]

The re-hearing a cause in equity can only be obtained while the decree is *in transitu* and incomplete; for after it has received the signature of the chancellor it can only be revised by supplemental bill. The method of obtaining a re-hearing is by entering a *caveat* with the proper officer, against the enrollment of the decree, and presenting a petition to the court requesting the indulgence of such re-hearing. This *caveat* proceeds upon the principle of preventing the inconvenience which has frequently been found to result from the too speedy signing of the decree; and it suspends the signature one lunar month from the time that it is presented to the judge for enrollment.

The petition must state particularly the objections which are conceived to lie against the decree, that the court may be competent to decide upon the propriety of the application, and if the whole decree is objected to, the case of the petitioners and the decretal part of the order are shortly set forth; and an intimation is given of the decree which the petitioners are advised ought to The orders of court require that a petition for re-hearing should be signed by two barristers, as a security that the application is not made for the purpose of delay.

---

[1] It would have been impracticable in a treatise of this nature to give an account of the practice in the different courts of the United States. It may be well to warn the student, that the English practice has been modified in this country, by local rules and statutes, and that the text can only be appealed to, as furnishing a general outline of the course of proceeding.

Form of a Petition for Re-Hearing.

To the Right Honorable the Lord High Chancellor of Great Britain.

In a cause wherein James Willis, by John Willis his father and next friend, is complainant, and Edward Willis and William Willis, are defendants.

The humble petition of the defendant showeth, that your petitioners find themselves much aggrieved by a decretal order made in this cause by your lordship, the —— day of ——, whereby your petitioner is ordered and directed to pay unto John Willis for the benefit of James Willis, an infant, the sum of £800, etc., such sum having been long since paid, and proof thereof made, as your petitioners conceive and are advised.

Your petitioners, therefore, humbly pray that your lordship will be pleased to vouchafe a re-hearing in this cause, before your lordship; they submitting to pay what costs the court shall award in case their complaint be found groundless; and your petitioners will pray, etc.

G. MADDOCKS.
A. STAINSBY.

This petition is left with the chancellor or the master of the rolls, who seldom refuses to subscribe his *fiat* for a re-hearing. Upon the re-hearing, all the evidence taken in the case, whether produced before or not, is now permitted to be read; for it is the decree of the same court which now sits only to hear reasons why it should not be enrolled and perfected; at which time, all omissions of either evidence or argument conductive to their information may be supplied.

The form of the decree upon a re-hearing differs from the first decree only by a recital of such other proceedings as have been since had in the cause, thus—

Whereas, by an order or decree of the right honorable,

the lord chancellor, made on the ——— day of ———, it was ordered and (reciting the first decree) with which order the defendant being dissatisfied, petitioned his lordship for a re-hearing of the said cause, and to have the order rectified in several particulars; and thereupon, by an order bearing date, etc., it was ordered that the said cause should be re-heard the ——— day of ———, upon the defendant's depositing £——— with the register; and the defendant deposited the said sum of £———, and the cause coming on to be heard in the presence of counsel, etc., the counsel for the defendant insisted that, etc. (here is set forth the substance of the defendants' arguments as recited in the order of re-hearing), whereas, the counsel for the plaintiff insisted that, etc. (the substance of the argument for the plaintiff;) whereupon, this court did declare and decree, that, etc. (as in the decree upon re-hearing). THURLOW, C.

WINTER, for the plaintiff.

No further obstacles can now be opposed to the enrollment of the decree, which is then completely perfected, and is deposited with the records of the court, there to remain *in perpetuam rei memoriam.*

CHAPTER XII.

OF THE EXECUTION OF DECREES.

THE decree being now perfected, a mandate of the court is awarded to enjoin its performance. It is a general principle, that the court of chancery has power to issue all process necessary to carry its decrees into effectual execution. When the decree is *in personam*, *i. e.*, directed against the person of the defendant, as for the payment of money, the process is a writ of execution, and upon its failure, a writ of sequestration.[1] But if the decree is

---

[1] The ancient method of compelling the observance of a decree, was by spending the whole process of the court, by attachment, proclamation, commission of rebellion, and sergeant-at-arms. But in the time of Chancellor Elesmere, a defendant having been taken upon one of the processes, and still retaining a sum of money which was decreed to the plaintiff, his lordship ordered a sequestration. About the latter end of the reign of Queen Anne, they began to shorten the process for compelling the execution of the decree; for, by beginning with the attachment, and proceeding to the commission of rebellion, a twelve-month elapsed before the plaintiff could receive any benefit from the decree, they, therefore, adopted the method of serving the defendant with a copy of the decree, and, upon his neglecting to obey it, he was ordered to be committed; and the practice was then immediately to commit him to the Fleet; and upon the return of *non est inventus*, by the warden of the Fleet, the court ordered a sequestration. But this being complained of by the sergeant-at-arms, as an infringement upon his accustomed privileges, an order was made in the seventh year of George I., that there should be no sequestration, but upon the return of *non est inventus* by that officer. Since which period the practice has been, either to issue successively the several processes of the court, or, upon service of the decree, to obtain an order that the defendant should be committed for disobedience; and upon that order move for a sergeant-at-arms, and a sequestration upon

in rem, i. e., against the lands of the defendant, it is usual after service of the writ of execution and attachment, to award an injunction to give the plaintiff possession. Where the decree directs deeds or other instruments to be executed by a party to the suit, the ordinary process of contempt must be employed to enforce their execution.

Form of a Writ of Execution of a Decree in Equity.

George the Third, etc., to Edward Willis and William Willis, greeting:

Whereas, by certain final judgment or decree, lately made before us in our court of chancery, in a certain cause there depending, wherein James Willis, an infant, by John Willis, his father and next friend, is complainant, and you, the said Edward Willis and William Willis, defendants: It is ordered and decreed, that, etc. (the decretal part of the order), as by the said decree duly enrolled, and remaining as of record, in our said court of chancery, doth and may fully appear:

Therefore, we strictly enjoin and command you, the said Edward Willis and William Willis, that you do, severally, pay, perform, fulfill, and execute all and every the moneys, matters, and things specified and contained in the said final judgment or decree, in all things so far as the same any way relates to or concerns you respect-

---

his return of *non est inventus*. This mode of shortening the process is justified, in the chief baron's opinion, by the ancient practice of immediately committing the defendant on disobedience to the order of the court, after having entered his appearance with the register; "for if a man can be committed for non-performance of an interlocutory order, when he has recorded his appearance, and departs in spite of the court, he certainly may be ordered to stand committed, after a decree pronounced for the appearance of the defendant is recorded at the hearing; or if the decree be pronounced in his absence, it is only conditional, and he is served with a copy of that decree, and acquiesces in it, before it can be absolute."

ively, according to the true meaning and import of the said decree, and of these presents; and hereof fail not at your peril. Witness ourself at Westminster, the —— day of ——, and in the 36th year of our reign.

COURTENAY.

Form of a Writ of Injunction to Deliver Possession of Land.

George the Third, etc., to Edward Willis, William Willis, and all other person or persons whatsoever, who are in possession of, or have, or claim, any right, title or interest whatsoever, of, in, or to, all or any part of the messuages, lands, tenements, or premises in question, greeting:

Whereas, it hath been represented to us in our court of chancery, in a cause wherein —— is plaintiff, and you the said Edward Willis and William Willis are defendants, that, by the decree made in this cause, it was ordered that you, the said defendants, should deliver possession of the premises in question, and all deeds and writings in your custody or power relating thereto, to the said complainant; that you, the said defendants, who are in possession of the messuages and lands in question were served with a writ of execution of the said decree, and have been required to deliver possession of the same, which you refuse to do, and a commission of rebellion having been issued against you, etc., it was ordered that an injunction be awarded against you, the said defendants, to enjoin you to deliver possession of the said messuages, and lands to the said complainant, pursuant to said decree.

We, therefore, in consideration of the premises, do strictly enjoin and command you, the said Edward Willis and William Willis, and both of you, and all and every other persons aforesaid, under the penalty of one thousand pounds to be levied upon your, each and every of your, lands, goods, and chattels, to our use, that you, each and every of you, do deliver the possession of the said messuages, lands, and premises, and of every part and parcel thereof, to the said ——, and hereof fail not at your peril.

Witness ourself at Westminster, the —— day of ——, in the 36th year of our reign.   Eliot.

CHAPTER XIII.

OF REVIEWING DECREES IN EQUITY.

IF after the enrollment of the decree, any new matter or evidence be discovered, which could not have been had or used when the decree was rendered; or if an apparent error of judgment appear on the face thereof, it may be reconsidered by means of a bill of review. A bill of review has been said to be in the nature of a writ of error, and its object is to procure an examination and alteration or reversal of a decree made upon a former bill, which decree has been signed and enrolled.

Where the bill of review is founded upon errors apparent on the face of the decree, it may be filed without leave of the court. But a bill of review founded upon newly discovered evidence, may be allowed or refused at the discretion of the court. And leave will not be granted until the party has actually rendered obedience to the decree, as far as it can be done without prejudicing the rights which he may seek to establish by the review, unless indeed in some special cases where the court will dispense with the immediate performance, upon the parties entering into sufficient security for its performance eventually.

Where the errors are apparent upon the face of the decree, the bill of review must be brought within the same period which limits writs of error at law; and the same rule applies without doubt as to the time which may elapse before it is filed after the discovery of new matter. But in reviewing a decree, no facts can be entered into which were before in issue, or which were known to the parties at the time of the former trial; for the same reason that no witnesses can be examined in a cause after publication, that is to say, an apprehension of perjury; and it must always be either for error appearing on the face of the decree, or upon some new matter, as a release, etc., "for unless it were confined to such new matter, it might be made use of as a method for a vexatious person to be oppressive to the other side, and for the cause never to be at rest."

This bill must recite the former bill, and the proceedings which have been had upon it; the former decree of the court; the points in which such decree is conceived to be erroneous; and the facts which have come to light since the former hearing;[1] after which it usually proceeds thus:

---

[1] The following form is borrowed from Blake's Chancery Practice:

Bill of Review.

To the honorable James Kent, chancellor of the State of New York:

Humbly complaining, showeth unto your honor, your orator A. B., of the city and county of New York, etc. [setting forth the former bill as in the decretal order], and thereupon the defendants answered; that the plaintiffs replied, and witnesses were examined and their depositions published, etc.; that the cause came on to hearing, and was heard and decreed by his honor, the chancellor, after which, etc., petitioned for a re-hearing to his honor, the chancellor, and the cause was accordingly re-heard, and a decree for the reversal was made by his honor, the chancellor; [set out the decree], and that the decree is signed and enrolled in this court; but your orator does aver and say, that he is aggrieved by the said last decree, and that he ought not to be bound thereby, nor should any such have been made or pronounced against your orator; neither ought your orator to pay, etc., as by the said decree is appointed; and that the said decree is erroneous, and ought to be reversed; and for error do, according to the course of this honorable court, assign the errors therein as followeth: First. Your orator says and hopes to maintain, that, etc., which is altogether uncertain, etc. Secondly. That, or which appears by, etc., to be fraudulent and corrupt. Thirdly. That, etc., was not alive at the time of the said decree made in the said cause against your orator, and so could not be bound by the said decree, and consequently your orator ought not

For all which errors and imperfections in the said decree, your orators have brought this their bill of review, and humbly conceive they should be relieved therein. In tender consideration whereof, and for that there are divers other errors and imperfections in said decree and proceedings, by reason whereof the same ought to be reviewed and reversed, added to, altered and amended, and that the said James Willis may answer the premises, and that your orator may be relieved in all and singular therein, according to equity and good conscience.

May it please, etc., (to grant subpena as in other cases.)

A. STAINSBY.

If the decree had been executed, the bill should pray for a further decree of the court, to put the complainant in his original situation.

To a bill of review for error apparent, the defendant seldom answers otherwise than by demurrer; "for that the said decree is free from the errors complained of."

A demurrer, however, rarely lies to the bill of review founded upon the discovery of new matter; for being exhibited only by leave of the court, the ground of it is generally well considered before it is brought.

This demurrer being set down to be argued, the court proceeds to reverse or affirm the former decree, and the

---

to be bound thereby; for all which said errors and imperfections in the said decree your orator has brought this his said bill of review, and humbly conceives he should be relieved therein. In tender consideration whereof, and for that there are divers other errors and imperfections in the said decree and proceedings, by reason whereof the same ought to be reviewed and reversed, altered, etc., and that the said, etc., may answer the premises; and that your orator may be relieved in all and singular the premises, according to equity and good conscience, etc. May it please your honor, to grant the most gracious writ of subpena of the people of the State of New York, issuing out of and under the seal of this honorable court, to be directed to, etc. Commanding him, etc.

prevailing party becomes entitled to the sum deposited, as security for costs.

Besides bills of review there are two other classes of bills which are exhibited subsequently to a decree, and which deserve notice, namely: bills to impeach a decree on account of fraud, and bills to carry decrees into execution. If a decree has been obtained by fraud, it may be impeached by original bill, without the leave of the court; the fraud used in obtaining the decree being the principal point at issue, and necessary to be established by proof before the propriety of the decree can be investigated. And where a decree has been thus obtained, the court will restore parties to their original situation, whatever their rights may be. A bill to set aside a decree for fraud, must state the decree, and the proceedings which led to it, with the circumstances of fraud on which it is impeached. The prayer must necessarily be varied according to the nature of the fraud used, and the extent of its operation in obtaining an improper decision of the court.

Sometimes from neglect of the parties, or other reason, it becomes impossible to carry a decree into execution, without the further order of the court. This happens generally, where the rights of parties under a decree have become so entangled and embarrassed, from their neglect to proceed under it, by subsequent events, that it is necessary to have the decree of the court to settle and ascertain them. The court in these cases does not ordinarily vary the original decree, but simply enforce it.

CHAPTER XIV.

OF APPEAL TO THE HOUSE OF LORDS.[1]

If either of the parties be dissatisfied with the decision of the court in which the suit has been prosecuted, they have yet a further resort, by appeal to the House of Lords. The decrees of the chancellor were originally final and conclusive. No appeal from his decision seems ever to have been allowed before 1581; but when courts of equity became the principal tribunals for deciding questions of property, it became obvious to the reason

---

[1] In the United States, the right of appeal is generally confined to final decrees. In England, however, there is no practical distinction upon this subject between final and interlocutory decrees. The right of appeal depends upon an arbitrary regulation, equally applicable to both kinds, to-wit: their enrollment. A decision of the chancellor which gives relief to any extent, or which settles a principle, may be brought at once before the House of Lords, if the decree or order has been enrolled; but the discussion in the appellate forum, is confined to the decree which is the subject of appeal, and can not be extended to any previous proceedings, however much the justice of the case may require it, without a formal extension of the right of appeal. There is, also, another difference between the English and American practice. An appeal, in England, does not of itself suspend proceedings upon the decree, without a special order to that effect, which is rarely granted. If the progress of a suit in chancery could be delayed by an appeal from any of the various interlocutory orders, which the circumstances of the case may require, it would become, as has been justly observed, the greatest judicial nuisance in the world; the arm of justice would be palsied; the whole business of the court of chancery be drawn into the court of last resort, before it had become ripe for discussion there; and thus not only render the voice of that court mute, and its process nugatory, but would destroy the appellate court itself, by overwhelming it with business.

of all mankind, that a revision of their decrees, by way of appeal, was as necessary as writs of error to the judgments of courts of law; and though the appellate jurisdiction was long and warmly controverted, it finally prevailed. The appeal is heard on a mere paper petition of the party, without any writ from the king, the foundation of which is said to be that this house, being the great court of the king, out of which the chancery was originally derived, petition will consequently bring the cause and record before them.

Form of Petition.

Between James Willis, by John Willis, his father and next friend, complainant, and Edward Willis and Wm. Willis, executors of the last will and testament of Thomas Atkins, Esq., deceased, defendants.

To the right honorable, the lords spiritual and temporal, in parliament assembled: The humble petition and appeal of the said defendants showeth,

That, etc. (setting forth the defendant's case). That the said complainant, James Willis, some time in or about Trinity term, 1785, exhibited his bill in the high court of chancery against your petitioners, to be relieved, etc. (the prayer of the bill.) To which bill your said petitioners appeared and answered; and thereby insisted, That, etc. (such parts of answer as the defendant alleged in rebuttal of the charges of plaintiff's bill). That the plaintiff having replied to the said answer, and your petitioners having rejoined, the said cause was at issue, and divers witnesses being examined on both sides, the same came on to be heard before the Lord Chancellor of Great Britain, the —— day of ——, 1785; when although your petitioners, by their said answer, and also divers witnesses by their depositions, did expressly swear, etc. (the facts sworn in the answer, and by the witnesses, and on the grounds of which the appeal is made), his lordship was pleased to decree, That, etc. (the decree and subsequent proceedings, if any, before the master). That your petitioners are advised that the said decree and subsequent orders are erroneous, and humbly appeal therefrom to your lordships.

Your petitioners therefore, humbly pray your lordships to grant to your petitioners your lordships' order of summons to the said complainant to put in his answer to this, your petitioners' appeal, at such time as your lordships shall prefix, in order that your lordships may hear the said cause; and that your lordships will please to reverse the said decree and subsequent orders in the said cause, or grant to your petitioners such relief in the premises as to your lordships, in your great wisdom, shall seem meet; and your petitioners shall ever pray, etc.

EDWARD WILLIS, } Appellants.
WILLIAM WILLIS,

A. Stainsby, } Counsel.
G. Maddocks,

This petition is lodged with the clerk of the house, and the respondent, being furnished with a copy, is ordered to put in his answer within a limited time.

The Form of Respondent's Answer.

The Answer of James Willis to the Petition and Appeal of Edward Willis and William Willis.

This respondent, not confessing or acknowledging all or any of the matters or things to be true, as in and by the said petition and appeal are mentioned and set forth, for answer thereto saith, that he believes it to be true that such decree as is complained of was made by the court of chancery, as in the said petition and appeal are mentioned and set forth; but, as to the dates, substance, and contents thereof, this respondent humbly craves leave to refer thereunto, when the same shall be produced; and this respondent humbly conceives, and is advised, that the said decree is agreeable to equity and justice, and therefore humbly hopes that the same will be affirmed and that the said petition and appeal will be dismissed this most honorable court, with costs.   A. MANNING.

The answer of the respondent having come in, a day is appointed, of which notice is given to the other party, for hearing the merits of the appeal. Upon a re-hearing or review, new matter, as we have seen, may be introduced; but no new evidence can be admitted upon an appeal to the house of lords. It is not the case of the same jurisdiction revising and correcting its own acts. It is a practice unknown to our law (though constantly followed in the spiritual courts), when a superior court is reviewing the sentence of an inferior, to examine the justice of the former decree by evidence that was never produced below.[1]

The cause being fully heard, their lordships " order and adjudge the said appeal to be dismissed," "the said decree to be reversed, and the bill of the said respondent

---

[1] The form of proceeding at the hearing of an appeal is prescribed by the house to be that "one of the counsel for the appellant shall open the cause; then the evidence on their side shall be read; which done, the other counsel of the appellants may make observations on the evidence; then one of the counsel for the respondent shall be heard, and the evidence on their side read; after which the other counsel for the respondents shall be heard, and one counsel only for the appellants' reply." Ord. 2 Mar. 1727. And printed copies of the respective cases of the appellant and respondent are usually delivered to the lords, previous to the day appointed for the hearing. And by Ord. 19, Ap. 1698, they are to be signed by the counsel retained in the cause, of which only two are allowed on each side in the house of lords, though any number may be engaged in the courts below.

to be dismissed," or pronounce such other decretal order, affirming, reversing, or varying the decree of the court below, as to their wisdom seems equitable. And this order being absolute and irrevocable, puts an end to our suit in equity.

RULES OF PRACTICE

FOR THE

Courts of Equity of the United States.

PROMULGATED BY THE SUPREME COURT OF THE UNITED STATES,
JANUARY TERM, 1842,

AND

THE ADDITIONAL RULES AND AMENDMENTS OF RULES,
ADOPTED AND PROMULGATED SINCE THAT TIME.

PRELIMINARY REGULATIONS.

1.

The circuit courts, as courts of equity, shall be deemed always open for the purpose of filing bills, answers, and other pleadings, for issuing and returning mesne and final process and commissions, and for making and directing all interlocutory motions, orders, rules, and other proceedings, preparatory to the hearing of all causes upon their merits.

2.

The clerk's office shall be open, and the clerk shall be in attendance thereon, on the first Monday of every month, for the purpose of receiving, entering, entertaining, and disposing of all motions, rules, orders, and other proceedings, which are grantable of course, and applied for, or had by the parties, or their solicitors, in all cases pending in equity, in pursuance of the rules hereby prescribed.

3.

Any judge of the circuit court, as well in vacation as in term, may, at chambers, or on the rule-days at the clerk's office, make and direct all such interlocutory orders, rules, and other proceedings, preparatory to the hearing of all causes upon their merits, in the same manner and with the same effect as the circuit court could make and direct the same in term, reasonable notice of the application therefor being first given to the adverse party, or his solicitor, to appear and show cause to the contrary at the next rule-day thereafter, unless some other time is assigned by the judge for the hearing.

4.

All motions, rules, orders, and other proceedings made and directed at chambers, or on rule-days at the clerk's office, whether special or of course, shall be entered by the clerk in an order-book, to be kept at the clerk's office, on the day when they are made and directed; which book shall be open at all office hours to the free inspection of the parties in any suit in equity, and their solicitors. And, except in cases where personal or other notice is specially required or directed, such entry in the order-book shall be deemed sufficient notice to the parties and their solicitors, without further service thereof, of all orders, rules, acts, notices, and other proceedings entered in such order-book, touching any and all the matters in the suits to and in which they are parties and solicitors. And notice to the solicitors shall be deemed notice to the parties for whom they appear and whom they represent, in all cases where personal notice on the parties is not otherwise specially required. Where the solicitors for all the parties in the suit reside in or near the same town or city, the judges of the circuit court may, by rule, abridge the time for notice of rules, orders, or other proceedings not requiring personal service on the parties, in their discretion.

5.

All motions and applications in the clerk's office for the issuing of mesne process and final process to enforce and execute decrees; for filing bills, answers, pleas, demurrers, and other pleadings; for making amendments to bills and answers; for making bills *pro confesso;* for filing exceptions, and for other proceedings in the clerk's office which do not, by the rules hereinafter described, require any allowance or order of the court, or of any judge thereof, shall be deemed motions and applications, grantable of course by the clerk of the court. But the same may be suspended, or altered, or rescinded by any judge of the court, upon special cause shown.

6.

All motions for rules or orders and other proceedings, which are not grantable of course, or without notice, shall, unless a different time be assigned by a judge of the court, be made on a rule-day, and entered in the order-book, and shall be heard at the rule-day next after that on which the motion is made. And if the adverse party, or his solicitor, shall not then appear, or shall not show good cause against the same, the motion may be heard by any judge of the court *ex parte*, and granted, as if not objected to, or refused, in discretion.

Process.

7.

The process of subpena shall constitute the proper mesne process in all suits in equity, in the first instance, to require the defendant to appear and answer the exigency of the bill; and, unless otherwise provided in these rules, or specially ordered by the circuit court, a writ of attachment, and, if the defendant can not be found, a writ of sequestration, or a writ of assistance to enforce a delivery of possesion, as the case may require, shall be the proper process to issue for the purpose of compelling obedience to any interlocutory or final order or decree of the court.

8.

Final process to execute any decree may, if the decree be solely for the payment of money, be by a writ of execution, in the form used in the circuit court in suits at common law in actions of *assumpsit*. If the decree be for the performance of any specific act, as, for example, for the execution of a conveyance of land or the delivering up of deeds, or other documents, the decree shall, in all cases, prescribe the time within which the act shall be done, of which the defendant shall be bound without further service to take notice; and upon affidavit of the plaintiff, filed in the clerk's office, that the same has not been complied with within the prescribed time, the clerk shall issue a writ of attachment against the delinquent party, from which, if attached thereon, he shall not be discharged, unless upon a full compliance with the decree and the payment of all costs, or upon a special order of the court or of a judge thereof, upon motion and affidavit, enlarging the time for the performance thereof. If the delinquent party can not be found, a writ of sequestration shall issue against his estate upon the return of *non est inventus*, to compel obedience to the decree.

9.

When any decree or order is for the delivery of possession upon proof made by affidavit of a demand and refusal to obey the decree or order, the party prosecuting the same shall be entitled to a writ of assistance from the clerk of the court.

10.

Every person, not being a party in any cause, who has obtained an order, or in whose favor an order shall have been made, shall be enabled to enforce obedience to such order by the same process as if he were a party to the cause; and every person, not being a party in any cause, against whom obedience to any order of the court may be enforced, shall be liable to the same process for enforcing obedience to such order as if he were the party in the cause.

Service of Process.

11.

No process of subpena shall issue from the clerk's office in any suit in equity until the bill is filed in the office.

12.

Whenever a bill is filed, the clerk shall issue the process of subpena thereon, as of course, upon the application of the plaintiff, which shall be returnable into the clerk's office the next rule-day, or the next rule-day but one, at the election of the plaintiff, occurring after twenty days from the time of the issuing thereof. At the bottom of the subpena shall be placed a memorandum, that the defendant is to enter his appearance in the suit in the clerk's office on or before the day at which the writ is returnable; otherwise, the bill may be taken *pro confesso*. Where there are more than one defendant, a writ of subpena may, at the election of the plaintiff, be sued out separately for each defendant, except in the case of husband and wife defendants, or a joint subpena against all the defendants.

13.

The service of all subpenas shall be by a delivery of a copy thereof by the officer serving the same to the defendant personally, or, in case of husband and wife, to the husband personally, or by leaving a copy thereof at the dwelling-house or usual place of abode of each defendant, with some free white person who is a member or resident in the family.

[*See Amendment, p.* 216.]

14.

Whenever any subpena shall be returned not executed as to any defendant, the plaintiff shall be entitled to another subpena, *toties quoties*, against such defendant, if he shall require it, until due service is made.

15.

The service of all process, mesne and final, shall be by the marshal of the district, or his deputy, or by some other person specially appointed by the court for that purpose, and not otherwise. In the latter case, the person serving the process shall make affidavit thereof.

16.

Upon the return of the subpena as served and executed upon any defendant, the clerk shall enter the suit upon his docket as pending in the court, and shall state the time of the entry.

Appearance.

17.

The appearance-day of the defendant shall be the rule-day to which the subpena is made returnable, provided he has been served with the process twenty days before that day; otherwise, his appearance-day shall be the next rule-day succeeding the rule-day when the process is returnable.

The appearance of the defendant, either personally or by his solicitor, shall be entered in the order-book on the day thereof by the clerk.

Bills taken Pro Confesso.

18.

It shall be the duty of the defendant, unless the time shall be otherwise enlarged, for cause shown, by a judge of the court, upon motion for that purpose, to file his plea, demurrer, or answer to the bill, in the clerk's office, on the rule-day next succeeding that of entering his appearance. In default thereof, the plaintiff may, at his election, enter an order (as of course) in the order-book, that the bill be taken *pro confesso;* and thereupon the cause shall be proceeded in *ex parte*, and the matter of the bill may be decreed by the court at the next ensuing term thereof accordingly, if the same can be done without an answer, and is proper to be decreed; or the plaintiff, if he requires any discovery or answer to enable him to obtain a proper decree, shall be entitled to process of attachment against the defendant, to compel an answer and the defendant shall not, when arrested upon such process, be discharged therefrom, unless upon filing his answer, or otherwise complying with such order as the court or a judge thereof may direct, as to pleading to or fully answering the bill, within a period to be fixed by the court or judge, and undertaking to speed the cause

19.

When the bill is taken *pro confesso*, the court may proceed to a decree at the next ensuing term thereof, and such decree rendered shall be deemed absolute, unless the court shall, at the same term, set aside the same or enlarge the time for filing the answer, upon cause shown upon motion and affidavit of the defendant. And no such motion shall be granted, unless upon the payment of the costs of the plaintiff in the suit up to that time, or such part thereof as the court shall deem reasonable, and unless the defendant shall undertake to file his answer within such time as the court shall direct, and submit to such other terms as the court shall direct, for the purpose of speeding the cause.

Frame of Bills.

20.

Every bill, in the introductory part thereof, shall contain the names, places of abode, and citizenship of all the parties, plaintiffs and defendants, by and against whom the bill is brought. The form, in substance, shall be as follows: "To the Judges of the Circuit Court of the United States for the district of ——: A. B., of ——, and a citizen of the State of ——, brings this his bill against C. D., of ——, and a citizen of the State of ——, and E. F., of ——, and a citizen of the State of ——. And thereupon your orator complains and says, that," etc.

21.

The plaintiff, in his bill, shall be at liberty to omit, at his option, the part which is usually called the common confederacy clause of the bill, averring a confederacy between the defendants to injure or defraud the plaintiff; also what is commonly called the charging part of the bill, setting forth the matters or excuses which the defendant is supposed to intend to set up by way of defense to the bill; also what is commonly called the jurisdiction clause of the bill, that the acts complained of are contrary to equity, and that the defendant is without any remedy at law; and the bill shall not be demurrable therefor. And the plaintiff may, in the narrative or stating part of his bill, state and avoid, by counter-averments, at his option, any matter or thing which he supposes will be insisted upon by the defendant by way of defense or excuse to the case made by the plaintiff for relief. The prayer of the bill shall ask the special relief to which the plaintiff supposes himself entitled, and also shall contain a prayer for general relief; and if an injunction, or a writ of *ne exeat regno*, or any other special order pending the suit, is required, it shall also be specially asked for.

22.

If any persons, other than those named as defendants in the bill, shall appear to be necessary or proper parties thereto, the bill shall aver the reason why they are not made parties, by showing them to be without the jurisdiction of the court, or that they can not be joined without ousting the jurisdiction of the court as to the other parties. And as to persons who are without the jurisdiction and may properly be made parties, the bill may pray that process may issue to make them parties to the bill if they should come within the jurisdiction.

23.

The prayer for process of subpena in the bill shall contain the names of all the defendants named in the introductory part of the bill, and if any of them are known to be infants under age, or otherwise under guardianship, shall state the fact, so that the court may take order thereon as justice may require, upon the return of the process. If an injunction, or a writ of *ne exeat regno*, or any other special order pending the suit, is asked for in the prayer for relief, that shall be sufficient without repeating the same in the prayer for process.

24.

Every bill shall contain the signature of counsel annexed to it, which shall be considered as an affirmation on his part, that upon the instructions given to him and the case laid before him, there is good ground for the suit, in the manner in which it is framed.

25.

In order to prevent unnecessary costs and expenses, and to promote brevity, succinctness, and directness in the allegations of bills and answers, the regular taxable costs for every bill and answer shall in no case exceed the sum which is allowed in the state court of chancery in the district, if any there be; but if there be none, then it shall not exceed the sum of three dollars for every bill or answer.

Scandal and Impertinence in Bills.

26.

Every bill shall be expressed in as brief and succinct terms as it reasonably can be, and shall contain no unnecessary recitals of deeds, documents, contracts, or other instruments, in *hæc verba*, or any other impertinent matter, or any scandalous matter not relevant to the suit. If it does, it may on exceptions be referred to a master by any judge of the court, for impertinence or scandal; and if so found by him, the matter shall be expunged at the expense of the plaintiff, and he shall pay to the defendant all his costs in the suit up to that time, unless the court or a judge thereof shall otherwise order. If the master shall report that the bill is not scandalous or impertinent, the plaintiff shall be entitled to all costs occasioned by the reference.

27.

No order shall be made by any judge for referring any bill, answer, or pleading, or other matter, or proceeding depending before the court for scandal or impertinence, unless exceptions are taken in writing and signed by counsel, describing the particular passages which are considered to be scandalous or impertinent; nor unless the exceptions shall be filed on or before the next rule-day after the process on the bill shall be returnable, or after the answer or pleading is filed. And such order, when obtained, shall be considered as abandoned, unless the party obtaining the order shall, without any unnecessary delay, procure the master to examine and report for the same on or before the next succeeding rule-day, or the master shall certify that further time is necessary for him to complete the examination.

Amendment of Bills.

28.

The plaintiff shall be at liberty, as a matter of course, and without payment of costs, to amend his bill in any matters whatsoever, before any copy has been taken out of the clerk's office, and in any small matters afterward, such as filling blanks, correcting errors of dates, misnomer of parties, mis-description of premises, clerical errors, and generally in matters of form. But if he amend in a material point (as he may do of course), after a copy has been so taken, before any answer or plea, or demurrer to the bill, he shall pay to the defendant the costs occasioned thereby, and shall, without delay, furnish him a fair copy thereof, free of expense, with suitable references to the places where the same are to be inserted. And if the amendments are numerous, he shall furnish in like manner to the defendant, a copy of the whole bill as amended; and if there be more than one defendant, a copy shall be furnished to each defendant affected thereby.

29.

After an answer, or plea, or demurrer is put in, and before replication, the plaintiff may, upon motion or petition, without notice, obtain an order from any judge of the court to amend his bill on or before the next succeeding rule-day, upon payment of costs or without payment of costs, as the court or a judge thereof may in his discretion direct. But after replication filed, the plaintiff shall not be permitted to withdraw it and to amend his bill, except upon a special order of a judge of the court, upon motion or petition, after due notice to the other party, and upon proof by affidavit that the same is not made for the purpose of vexation or delay, or that the matter of the proposed amendment is material, and could not with reasonable diligence have been sooner introduced into the bill, and upon the plaintiff's submitting to such other terms as may be imposed by the judge for speeding the cause.

30.

If the plaintiff, so obtaining any order to amend his bill after answer, or plea, or demurrer, or after replication, shall not file his amendments or amended bill, as the case may require, in the clerk's office, on or before the next succeeding rule-day, he shall be considered to have abandoned the same, and the cause shall proceed as if no application for any amendment had been made.

Demurrers and Pleas.

31.

No demurrer or plea shall be allowed to be filed to any bill, unless upon a certificate of counsel, that in his opinion it is well founded in point of law, and supported by the affidavit of the defendant, that it is not interposed for delay; and if a plea, that it is true in point of fact.

32.

The defendant may, at any time before the bill is taken for confessed, or afterward with the leave of the court, demur or plead to the whole bill, or to part of it, and he may demur to part, plead to part, and answer as to the residue; but in every case in which the bill specially charges fraud or combination, a plea to such part must be accompanied with an answer fortifying the plea, and explicitly denying the fraud and combination, and the facts on which the charge is founded.

33.

The plaintiff may set down the demurrer or plea to be argued, or he may take issue on the plea. If, upon an issue, the facts stated in the plea be determined for the defendant, they shall avail him as far as in law and equity they ought to avail him.

34.

If, upon the hearing, any demurrer or plea is overruled, the plaintiff shall be entitled to his costs in the cause up to that period, unless the court shall be satisfied that the defendant had good ground in point of law or fact to interpose the same, and it was not interposed vexatiously, or for delay. And upon the overruling of any plea or demurrer, the defendant shall be assigned to answer the bill, or so much thereof as is covered by the plea or demurrer, the next succeeding rule-day, or at such other period as, consistently with justice and the rights of the defendant, the same can, in the judgment of the court, be reasonably done; in default whereof, the bill shall be taken against him, *pro confesso*, and the matter thereof proceeded in and decreed accordingly.

35.

If, upon the hearing, any demurrer or plea shall be allowed, the defendant shall be entitled to his costs. But the court may, in its discretion, upon motion of the plaintiff, allow him to amend his bill upon such terms as it shall deem reasonable.

36.

No demurrer or plea shall be held bad and overruled upon argument, only because such demurrer or plea shall not cover so much of the bill as it might by law have extended to.

37.

No demurrer or plea shall be held bad and overruled upon argument, only because the answer of the defendant may extend to some part of the same matter as may be covered by such demurrer or plea.

38.

If the plaintiff shall not reply to any plea, or set down any plea or demurrer for argument, on the rule-day when the same is filed, or on the next succeeding rule-day, he shall be deemed to admit the truth and sufficiency thereof, and his bill shall be dismissed as of course, unless a judge of the court shall allow him further time for the purpose.

Answers.

39.

The rule, that if a defendant submits to answer he shall answer fully to all the matters of the bill, shall no longer apply in cases where he might by plea protect himself from such answer and discovery. And the defendant shall be entitled in all cases by answer to insist upon all matters of defense (not being matters of abatement or to the character of the parties, or matters of form) in bar of or to the merits of the bill, of which he may be entitled to avail himself by a plea in bar; and in such answer he shall not be compellable to answer any other matters than he would be compellable to answer and discover upon filing a plea in bar, and an answer in support of such plea, touching the matters set forth in the bill, to avoid or repel the bar or defense. Thus, for example, a bona fide purchaser, for a valuable consideration, without notice, may set up that defense by way of answer instead of plea, and shall be entitled to the same protection, and shall not be compellable to make any further answer or discovery of his title than he would be in any answer in support of such plea.

40.

A defendant shall not be bound to answer any statement or charge in the bill, unless specially and particularly interrogated thereto; and a defendant shall not be bound to answer any interrogatory in the bill, except those interrogatories which such defendant is required to answer; and where a defendant shall answer any statement or charge in the bill, to which he is not interrogated, only by stating his ignorance of the matter so stated or charged, such answer shall be deemed impertinent.

[*This rule was repealed and annulled, December Term,* 1850. *See page* 214.]

41.

The interrogatories contained in the interrogating part of the bill shall be divided as conveniently as may be from each other, and numbered consecutively 1, 2, 3, etc.; and the interrogatories which each defendant is required to answer shall be specified in a note at the foot of the bill, in the form or to the effect following; that is to say—"The defendant (A. B.) is required to answer the interrogatories numbered respectively 1, 2, 3, etc.;" and the office copy of the bill taken by each defendant shall not contain any interrogatories except those which such defendant is so required to answer, unless such defendant shall require to be furnished with a copy of the whole bill.

[*See Amendment, p.* 215.]

42.

The note at the foot of the bill, specifying the interrogatories which each defendant is required to answer, shall be considered and treated as part of the bill, and the addition of any such note to the bill, or any alteration in, or addition to, such note after the bill is filed, shall be considered and treated as an amendment of the bill.

43.

Instead of the words of the bill now in use, preceding the interrogating part thereof, and beginning with the words "To the end, therefore," there shall hereafter be used words in the form or to the effect following: "To the end, therefore, that the said defendants may, if they can, show why your orator should not have the relief hereby prayed, and may, upon their several and respective corporal oaths, and according to the best and utmost of their several and respective knowledge, remembrance, information, and belief, full, true, direct, and perfect answer make to such of the several interrogatories hereinafter numbered and set forth, as by the note hereunder written they are respectively required to answer; that is to say—

"1. Whether, etc.

"2. Whether, etc."

44.

A defendant shall be at liberty, by answer, to decline answering any interrogatory, or part of an interrogatory, from answering which he might have protected himself by demurrer; and he shall be at liberty so to decline, notwithstanding he shall answer other parts of the bill, from which he might have protected himself by demurrer.

45.

No special replication to any answer shall be filed. But if any matter alleged in the answer shall make it necessary for the plaintiff to amend his bill, he may have leave to amend the same with or without the payment of costs, as the court, or a judge thereof, may in his discretion direct.

46.

In every case where an amendment shall be made after answer filed, the defendant shall put in a new or supplemental answer, on or before the next succeeding rule-day after that on which the amendment or amended bill is filed, unless the time is enlarged or otherwise ordered by a judge of the court; and upon his default the like proceedings may be had as in cases of an omission to put in an answer.

Parties to Bills.

47.

In all cases where it shall appear to the court that persons, who might otherwise be deemed necessary or proper parties to the suit, can not be made parties by reason of their being out of the jurisdiction of the court, or incapable otherwise of being made parties, or because their joinder would oust the jurisdiction of the court as to the parties before the court, the court may in their discretion proceed in the cause without making such persons parties; and in such cases the decree shall be without prejudice to the rights of the absent parties.

48.

Where the parties on either side are very numerous, and can not, without manifest inconvenience and oppressive delays in the suit, be all brought before it, the court in its discretion may dispense with making all of them parties, and may proceed in the suit, having sufficient parties before it to represent all the adverse interests of the plaintiffs and the defendants in the suit properly before it. But in such cases the decree shall be without prejudice to the rights and claims of all the present parties.

49.

In all suits concerning real estate, which is vested in trustees by devise, and such trustees are competent to sell and give discharge for the proceeds of the sale, and for the rents and profits of the estate, such trustees shall represent the persons beneficially interested in the estate, or the proceeds, or the rents and profits, in the same manner, and to the same extent, as the executors or administrators in suits concerning personal estate represent the persons beneficially interested in such personal estate; and in such cases it shall not be necessary to make the persons beneficially interested in such real estate, or rents and profits, parties to the suit; but the court may, upon consideration of the matter on the hearing, if it shall so think fit, order such persons to be made parties.

50.

In suits to execute the trusts of a will, it shall not be necessary to make the heir-at-law a party; but the plaintiff shall be at liberty to make the heir-at-law a party where he desires to have the will established against him.

51.

In all cases in which the plaintiff has a joint and several demand against several persons, either as principals or sureties, it shall not be necessary to bring before the court, as parties to a suit concerning such demand, all the persons liable thereto; but the plaintiff may proceed against one or more of the persons severally liable.

52.

Where the defendant shall, by his answer, suggest that the bill is defective for want of parties, the plaintiff shall be at liberty, within fourteen days after answer filed, to set down the cause for argument upon that objection only; and the purpose for which the same is so set down shall be notified by an entry, to be made in the clerk's order book, in the form or to the effect following, (that is to say,) "Set down upon defendant's objection for want of parties." And where the plaintiff shall not so set down his cause, but shall proceed therewith to a hearing, notwithstanding an objection for want of parties taken by the answer, he shall not, at the hearing of the cause, if the defendant's objection shall then be allowed, be entitled, as of course, to an order for liberty to amend his bill by adding parties. But the court, if it thinks fit, shall be at liberty to dismiss the bill.

53.

If a defendant shall, at the hearing of a cause, object that a suit is defective for want of parties not having by plea or answer taken the objection, and therein specified by name or description the parties to whom the objection applies, the court (if it shall think fit) shall be at liberty to make a decree saving the rights of the absent parties.

Nominal Parties to Bills.

54.

Where no account, payment, conveyance, or other direct relief is sought against a party to a suit, not being an infant, the party, upon service of the subpena upon him, need not appear and answer the bill, unless the plaintiff specially requires him so to do by the prayer of his bill; but he may appear and answer at his option; and if he does not appear and answer he shall be bound by all the proceedings in the cause. If the plaintiff shall require him to appear and answer, he shall be entitled to the costs of all the proceedings against him, unless the court shall otherwise direct.

55.

Whenever an injunction is asked for by the bill to stay proceedings at law, if the defendant do not enter his appearance and plead, demur, or answer to the same within the time prescribed therefor by these rules, the plaintiff shall be entitled, as of course, upon motion without notice, to such injunction. But special injunctions shall be grantable only upon due notice to the other party by the court in term, or by a judge thereof in vacation, after a hearing, which may be *ex parte*, if the adverse party does not appear at the time and place ordered. In every case where an injunction, either the common injunction or a special injunction, is awarded in vacation, it shall, unless previously dissolved by the judge granting the same, continue until the next term of the court, or until it is dissolved by some other order of the court.

Bills of Revivor and Supplemental Bills.

56.

Whenever a suit in equity shall become abated by the death of either party, or by any other event, the same may be revived by a bill of revivor, or a bill in the nature of a bill of revivor, as the circumstances of the case may require, filed by the proper parties entitled to revive the same; which bill may be filed in the clerk's office at any time; and upon suggestion of the facts, the proper process of subpena shall, as of course, be issued by the clerk, requiring the proper representatives of the other party to appear and show cause, if any they have, why the cause should not be revived. And if no cause shall be shown at the next rule-day which shall occur after fourteen days from the time of the service of the same process, the suit shall stand revived, as of course.

57.

Whenever any suit in equity shall become defective, from any event happening after the filing of the bill (as, for example, by change of interest in the parties), or for any other reason a supplemental bill, or a bill in the nature of a supplemental bill, may be necessary to be filed in the cause, leave to file the same may be granted by any judge of the court on any rule-day, upon proper cause shown, and due notice to the other party. And if leave is granted to file such supplemental bill, the defendant shall demur, plead, or answer thereto, on the next succeeding rule-day after the supplemental bill is filed in the clerk's office, unless some other time shall be assigned by a judge of the court.

58.

It shall not be necessary in any bill of revivor or supplemental bill to set forth any of the statements in the original suit, unless the special circumstances of the case may require it.

Answers.

59.

Every defendant may swear to his answer before any justice or judge of any court of the United States, or before any commissioner appointed by any circuit court to take testimony or depositions, or before any master in chancery appointed by any circuit court, or before any judge of any court of a state or territory.

Amendment of Answers.

60.

After an answer is put in, it may be amended as of course, in any matter of form, or by filling up a blank, or correcting a date, or reference to a document or other small matter, and be re-sworn, at any time before a replication is put in, or the cause is set down for a hearing upon bill and answer. But after replication, or such setting down for a hearing, it shall not be amended in any material matters, as by adding new facts or defenses, or qualifying or altering the original statements, except by special leave of the court or of a judge thereof, upon motion and cause shown after due notice to the adverse party, supported, if required, by affidavit. And in every case where leave is so granted, the court or the judge granting the same may, in his discretion, require that the same be separately engrossed and added as a distinct amendment to the original answer, so as to be distinguishable therefrom.

Exceptions to Answers.

61.

After an answer is filed on any rule-day, the plaintiff shall be allowed until the next succeeding rule-day to file in the clerk's office exceptions thereto for insufficiency, and no longer, unless a longer time shall be allowed for the purpose, upon cause shown to the court or a judge thereof; and if no exception shall be filed thereto within that period, the answer shall be deemed and taken to be sufficient.

62.

When the same solicitor is employed for two or more defendants, and separate answers shall be filed, or other proceedings had by two or more of the defendants separately, costs shall not be allowed for such separate answers or other proceedings, unless a master, upon reference to him, shall certify that such separate answers and other proceedings were necessary or proper, and ought not to have been joined together.

63.

Where exceptions shall be filed to the answer for insufficiency within the period prescribed by these rules, if the defendant shall not submit to the same and file an amended answer on the next succeeding rule-day, the plaintiff shall forthwith set them down for a hearing on the next succeeding rule-day thereafter before a judge of the court, and shall enter, as of course, in the order-book, an order for that purpose. And if he shall not so set down the same for a hearing, the exceptions shall be deemed abandoned, and the answer shall be deemed sufficient; provided, however, that the court, or any judge thereof, may, for good cause shown, enlarge the time for filing exceptions, or for answering the same, in his discretion, upon such terms as he may deem reasonable.

64.

If at the hearing the exceptions shall be allowed, the defendant shall be bound to put in a full and complete answer thereto on the next succeeding rule-day; otherwise the plaintiff shall, as of course, be entitled to take the bill, so far as the matter of such exceptions is concerned, as confessed, or, at his election, he may have a writ of attachment to compel the defendant to make a better answer to the matter of the exceptions; and the defendant, when he is in custody upon such writ, shall not be discharged therefrom but by an order of the court, or of a judge thereof, upon his putting in such answer and complying with such other terms as the court or judge may direct.

65.

If, upon argument, the plaintiff's exceptions to the answer shall be overruled, or the answer shall be adjudged insufficient, the prevailing party shall be entitled to all the costs occasioned thereby, unless otherwise directed by the court, or the judge thereof, at the hearing upon the exceptions.

Replication and Issue.

66.

Whenever the answer of the defendant shall not be excepted to, or shall be adjudged or deemed sufficient, the plaintiff shall file the general replication thereto on or before the next succeeding rule-day thereafter; and in all cases where the general replication is filed the cause shall be deemed to all intents and purposes at issue, without any rejoinder or other pleading on either side.

If the plaintiff shall omit or refuse to file such replication within the prescribed period, the defendant shall be entitled to an order, as of course, for a dismissal of the suit; and the suit shall thereupon stand dismissed, unless the court, or a judge thereof, shall, upon motion for cause shown, allow a replication to be filled *nunc pro tunc*, the plaintiff submitting to speed the cause, and to such other terms as may be directed.

Testimony—How Taken.

67.

After the cause is at issue, commissions to take testimony may be taken out in vacation as well as in term, jointly by both parties, or severally by either party, upon interrogatories filed by the party taking out the same in the clerk's office, ten days' notice thereof being given to the adverse party to file cross-interrogatories before the issuing of the commission; and if no cross-interrogatories are filed at the expiration of the time, the commission may issue *ex parte*. In all cases the commissioner or commissioners shall be named by the court, or by a judge thereof. If the parties shall so agree, the testimony may be taken upon oral interrogatories by the parties or their agents, without filing any written interrogatories.

December Term, 1854.

Ordered, That the sixty-seventh rule governing equity practice be so amended as to allow the presiding judge of any court exercising jurisdiction, either in term time or vacation, to vest in the clerk of said court general power to name commissioners to take testimony in like manner that the court or judge thereof can now do by the said sixty-seventh rule.

December Term, 1861.

Ordered, That the last paragraph in the sixty-seventh rule in equity be repealed, and the rule be amended as follows: Either party may give notice to the other that he desires the evidence to be adduced in the cause to be taken orally, and thereupon all the witnesses to be examined shall be examined before one of the examiners of the court, or before an examiner to be specially appointed by the court, the examiner to be furnished with a copy of the bill and answer, if any; and such examination shall take place in the presence of the parties or their agents, by their counsel or solicitors, and the witnesses shall be subject to cross-examination, and re-examination, and which shall be conducted as near as may be in the mode now used in common law courts. The depositions taken upon such oral examination shall be taken down in writing by the examiner in the form of narrative, unless he determines the examination shall be by question and answer in special instances; and, when completed, shall be read over to the witness and signed by him in the presence of the parties or counsel, or such of them as may attend; provided, if the witness shall refuse to sign the said deposition, then the examiner shall sign the same; and the examiner may upon all examinations state any special matters to the court as he shall think fit; and any question or questions which may be objected to shall be noted by the examiner upon the deposition, but he shall not have power to decide on the competency, materiality, or relevancy of the questions; and the court shall have power to deal with the costs of incompetent, immaterial, or irrelevant depositions, or parts of them, as may be just.

The Compulsory Attendance of Witnesses.

In case of refusal of witnesses to attend, to be sworn, or to answer any question put by the examiner, or by counsel or solicitor, the same practice shall be adopted as is now practiced with respect to witnesses to be produced on examination before an examiner of said court on written interrogatories.

Notice shall be given by the respective counsel or solicitors, to the opposite counsel or solicitors or parties, of the time and place of the examination, for such reasonable time as the examiner may fix by order in each cause.

When the examination of witnesses before the examiner is concluded, the original deposition, authenticated by the signature of the examiner, shall be transmitted by him to the clerk of the court, to be there filed of record in the same mode as prescribed in the thirtieth section of act of Congress, September 24, 1789.

Testimony may be taken on commission in the usual way by written interrogatories and cross-interrogatories, on motion to the court in term time, or to a judge in vacation, for special reasons satisfactory to the court or judge.

December Term, 1869.

Ordered, Where the evidence to be adduced in a cause is to be taken orally, as provided in the order passed at the December term, 1861, amending the 67th General Rule, the court may, on motion of either party, assign a time within which the complainant shall take his evidence in support of the bill, and a time thereafter within which the defendant shall take his evidence in defense, and a time thereafter within which the complainant shall take his evidence in reply; and no further evidence shall be taken in the cause unless by agreement of the parties, or by leave of the court first obtained on motion for cause shown.

68.

Testimony may also be taken in the cause, after it is at issue, by deposition, according to the acts of Congress. But in such case, if no notice is given to the adverse party of the time and place of taking the deposition, he shall, upon motion and affidavit of the fact, be entitled to a cross-examination of the witness either under a commission or by a new deposition taken under the acts of Congress, if a court or a judge thereof shall, under all the circumstances, deem it reasonable.

69.

Three months, and no more, shall be allowed for the taking of testimony after the cause is at issue, unless the court or a judge thereof shall, upon special cause shown by either party, enlarge the time; and no testimony taken after such period shall be allowed to be read in evidence at the hearing. Immediately upon the return of the commissions and depositions containing the testimony into the clerk's office, publication thereof may be ordered in the clerk's office by any judge of the court, upon due notice to the parties, or it may be enlarged, as he may deem reasonable under all the circumstances. But, by consent of the parties, publication of the testimony may at any time pass in the clerk's office, such consent being in writing, and a copy thereof entered in the order-books, or indorsed upon the deposition or testimony.

Testimony de bene esse.

70.

After any bill filed, and before the defendant hath answered the same, upon affidavit made that any of the plaintiff's witnesses are aged and infirm, or going out of the country, or that any one of them is a single witness to a material fact, the clerk of the court shall, as of course, upon the application of the plaintiff, issue a commission to such commissioner or commissioners, as a judge of the court may direct, to take the examination of such witness or witnesses *de bene esse*, upon giving due notice to the adverse party of the time and place of taking his testimony.

Form of the Last Interrogatory.

71.

The last interrogatory in the written interrogatories to take testimony now commonly in use shall in the future be altered, and stated in substance thus: "Do you know, or can you set forth, any other matter or thing which may be a benefit or advantage to the parties at issue in this cause, or either of them, or that may be material to the subject of this your examination, or the matters in question in this cause? If yea, set forth the same fully and at large in your answer."

Cross-bill.

72.

Where a defendant in equity files a cross-bill for discovery only against the plaintiff in the original bill, the defendant to the original bill shall first answer thereto, before the original plaintiff shall be compellable to answer the cross-bill. The answer of the original plaintiff to such cross-bill may be read and used by the party filing the cross-bill at the hearing, in the same manner and under the same restrictions as the answer praying relief may now be read and used.

Reference to and Proceedings before Masters.

73.

Every decree for an account of the personal estate of a testator or intestate shall contain a direction to the master, to whom it is referred to take the same, to inquire and state to the court what parts, if any, of such personal estate are outstanding or undisposed of, unless the court shall otherwise direct.

74.

Whenever any reference of any matter is made to a master to examine and report thereon, the party at whose instance, or for whose benefit, the reference is made, shall cause the same to be presented to the master for a hearing on or before the next rule-day succeeding the time when the reference was made; if he shall omit to do so, the adverse party shall be at liberty forthwith to cause proceedings to be had before the master at the costs of the party procuring the reference.

75.

Upon every such reference it shall be the duty of the master, as soon as he reasonably can after the same is brought before him, to assign a time and place for proceedings in the same, and to give due notice thereof to each of the parties or their solicitors; and if either party shall fail to appear at the time and place appointed, the master shall be at liberty to proceed *ex parte*, or, in his discretion, to adjourn the examination and proceedings to a future day, giving notice to the absent party or his solicitor of such adjournment; and it shall be the duty of the master to proceed with all reasonable diligence in every such reference, and with the least practicable delay, and either party shall be at liberty to apply to the court, or a judge thereof, for an order to the master to speed the proceedings, and to make his report, and to certify to the court or judge the reasons for any delay.

76.

In the reports made by the master to the court no part of any state of facts, charge, affidavit, deposition, examination or answer, brought in or used before them, shall be stated or recited. But such state of facts, charge, affidavit, deposition, examination, or answer, shall be identified, specified, and referred to, so as to inform the court what state of facts, charge, affidavit, deposition, examination, or answer, were so brought in or used.

77.

The master shall regulate all the proceedings in every hearing before him, upon every such reference; and he shall have full authority to examine the parties in the cause, upon oath, touching all matters contained in the reference; and also to require the production of all books, papers, writings, vouchers, and other documents applicable thereto; and also to examine on oath, *viva voce*, all witnesses produced by the parties before him, and to order the examination of other witnesses to be taken, under a commission to be issued upon his certificate from the clerk's office, or by deposition, according to the acts of Congress, or otherwise, as hereinafter provided; and also to direct the mode in which the matters requiring evidence shall be proved before him; and generally to do all other acts, and direct all other inquiries and proceedings in the matters before him, which he may deem necessary and proper to the justice and merits thereof and the rights of the parties.

78.

Witnesses who live within the district may, upon due notice to the opposite party, be summoned to appear before the commissioner appointed to take testimony, or before a master or examiner appointed in any cause, by subpena in the usual form, which may be issued by the clerk in blank, and filled up by the party praying the same, or by the commissioner, master, or examiner, requiring the attendance of the witnesses at the time and place specified, who shall be allowed for attendance the same compensation as for attendance in court; and if any witness shall refuse to appear, or to give evidence, it shall be deemed a contempt of the court, which being certified to the clerk's office by the commissioner, master, or examiner, an attachment may issue thereupon by order of the court, or of any judge thereof, in the same manner as if the contempt were for not attending, or for refusing to give testimony in the court. But nothing herein contained shall prevent the examination of witnesses *viva voce* when produced in open court, if the court shall, in its discretion, deem it advisable.

79.

All parties accounting before a master, shall bring in their respective accounts in the form of debtor and creditor; and any of the other parties who shall not be satisfied with the accounts so brought in shall be at liberty to examine the accounting party *viva voce*, or upon interrogatories in the master's office, or by deposition, as the master shall direct.

80.

All affidavits, depositions, and documents which have been previously made, read, or used in the court, upon any proceeding in any cause or matter, may be used before the master.

81.

The master shall be at liberty to examine any creditor or other person coming in to claim before him, either upon written interrogatories, or *viva voce*, or in both modes, as the nature of the case may appear to him to require. The evidence upon such examinations shall be taken down by the master, or by some other person by his order and in his presence, if either party requires it, in order that the same may be used by the court, if necessary.

82.

The circuit courts may appoint standing masters in chancery in their respective districts, both the judges concurring in the appointment; and they may also appoint a master *pro hac vice* in any particular case. The compensation to be allowed to every master in chancery for his services in any particular case shall be fixed by the circuit court in its discretion, having regard to all the circumstances thereof, and the compensation shall be charged upon and borne by such of the parties in the cause as the court shall direct. The master shall not retain his report as security for his compensation; but when the compensation is allowed by the court, he shall be entitled to an attachment for the amount against the party who is ordered to pay the same, if, upon notice thereof, he does not pay it within the time prescribed by the court.

Exceptions to Report of Master.

83.

The master, as soon as his report is ready, shall return the same into the clerk's office, and the day of the return shall be entered by the clerk in the order-book. The parties shall have one month from the time of filing the report to file exceptions thereto; and if no exceptions are within that period filed by either party, the report shall stand confirmed on the next rule-day after the month is expired. If exceptions are filed, they shall stand for hearing before the court, if the court is then in session; or, if not, then at the next sitting of the court which shall be held thereafter by adjournment or otherwise.

84.

And in order to prevent exceptions to reports from being filed for frivolous causes, or for mere delay, the party whose exceptions are overruled shall, for every exception overruled, pay costs to the other party, and for every exception allowed shall be entitled to costs—the costs to be fixed in each case by the court, by a standing rule of the circuit court.

Decrees.

85.

Clerical mistakes in decrees, or decretal orders, or errors arising from any accidental slip or omission, may, at any time before an actual enrollment thereof, be corrected by order of the court or judge thereof, upon petition, without the form or expense of a re-hearing.

86.

In drawing up decrees and orders, neither the bill, nor answer, nor other pleadings, nor any part thereof, nor the report of any master, nor any other prior proceeding, shall be recited or stated in the decree or order; but the decree and order shall begin, in substance, as follows: "This cause came on to be heard (or to be further heard, as the case may be) at this term, and was argued by counsel; and thereupon, upon consideration thereof, it was ordered, adjudged, and decreed as follows, viz:" (Here insert the decree or order.)

Guardians and Prochein Amis.

87.

Guardians *ad litem* to defend a suit may be appointed by the court, or by any judge thereof, for infants or other persons who are under guardianship, or otherwise incapable to sue for themselves. All infants and other persons so incapable may sue by their guardians, if any, or by their *prochein ami;* subject, however, to such orders as the court may direct for the protection of infants and other persons.

88.

Every petition for a re-hearing shall contain the special matter or cause on which such re-hearing is applied for, shall be signed by counsel, and the facts therein stated, if not apparent on the record, shall be verified by the oath of the party, or by some other person. No re-hearing shall be granted after the term at which the final decree of the court shall have been entered and recorded, if an appeal lies to the supreme court. But if no appeal lies, the petition may be admitted at any time before the end of the next term of the court in the discretion of the court.

89.

The circuit courts (both judges concurring therein) may make any other and further rules and regulations for the practice, proceedings, and process, mesne and final, in their respective districts, not inconsistent with the rules hereby prescribed, in their discretion, and from time to time alter and amend the same.

90.

In all cases where the rules prescribed by this court, or by the circuit court, do not apply, the practice of the circuit court shall be regulated by the present practice of the high court of chancery in England, so far as the same may reasonably be applied consistently with the circumstances and local convenience of the district where the court is held, not as positive rules, but as furnishing just analogies to regulate the practice.

91.

Whenever, under these rules, an oath is or may be required to be taken, the party may, if conscientiously scrupulous of taking an oath, in lieu thereof, make solemn affirmation to the truth of the facts stated by him.

92.

These rules shall take effect, and be in force, in all the circuit courts of the United States, from and after the first day of August next; but they may be previously adopted by any circuit court in its discretion, and when and as soon as these rules shall so take effect and be of force, the rules of practice for the circuit courts in equity suits, promulgated and prescribed by this court in March, 1822, shall henceforth cease, and be of no further force or effect. And the clerk of this court is directed to have these rules printed, and to transmit a printed copy thereof, duly certified, to the clerks of the several courts of the United States, and to each of the judges thereof.

December Term, 1850.

93.

Ordered, That the fortieth rule heretofore adopted and promulgated by this court as one of the rules of practice in suits in equity in the circuit courts be, and the same is hereby, repealed and annulled. And it shall not hereafter be necessary to interrogate a defendant specially and particularly upon any statement in the bill, unless the complainant desires to do so, to obtain a discovery.

December Term, 1863.

94.

Ordered, That in suits in equity for the foreclosure of mortgages in the circuit courts of the United States, or in any court of the territories having jurisdiction of the same, a decree may be rendered for any balance that may be found due to the complainant over and above the proceeds of the sale or sales, and execution may issue for the collection of the same, as is provided in the 8th rule of this court regulating the equity practice, where the decree is solely for the payment of money.[1]

95.

Amendment to the 41st Rule.

If the complainant, in his bill, shall waive an answer under oath, or shall only require an answer under oath with regard to certain specified interrogatories, the answer of the defendant, though under oath, except such part thereof as shall be directly responsive to such interrogatories, shall not be evidence in his favor, unless the cause be set down for hearing on the bill and answer only; but may, nevertheless, be used as an affidavit, with the same effect as heretofore, on a motion to grant or dissolve an injunction, or on any other incidental motion in the cause; but this shall not prevent a defendant from becoming a witness in his behalf, under section 3 of the act of Congress of July 2, 1864. [*Promulgated May* 6, 1872.]

---

[1] 1 Wall. 7.

96.

Amendment to the 13th Rule.

The 13th rule of practice in equity is amended so that it will read as follows: "The service of all subpenas shall be by a delivery of a copy thereof by the officer serving the same to the defendant personally, or by leaving a copy thereof at the dwelling-house or usual place of abode of each defendant, with some adult person who is a member or resident in the family." [*Promulgated May* 3, 1875.]

RULES OF THE UNITED STATES SUPREME COURT, DE-DEMBER TERM, 1858, AFFECTING EQUITY PRACTICE.

3.

This court consider the practice of the Court of the King's [Queen's] Bench and of chancery, in England, as affording outlines for the practice of this court; and they will from time to time make such alterations therein as circumstances may render necessary.

5.

All process in this court shall be in the name of the President of the United States.

When process at common law or in equity shall issue against a state, the same shall be served on the governor, or chief executive magistrate, and attorney-general, of such state.

Process of *subpena* issuing out of the court in any suit in equity, shall be served on the defendant sixty days before the return day of said process; and if the defendant, on such service of the *subpena*, shall not appear at the return day contained therein, the complainant shall be at liberty to proceed *ex parte*.

12.

In all cases where further proof is ordered by the court, the depositions which shall be taken shall be by a commission to be issued from the court, or from any circuit court of the United States.

13.

In all cases of equity and admiralty jurisdiction heard in this court, no objection shall hereafter be allowed to be taken to the admissibility of any deposition, deed, grant, or other exhibit found in the record, as evidence, unless objection was taken thereto in the court below, and entered of record; but the same shall otherwise be deemed to have been admitted by consent.

LAWS OF THE UNITED STATES

RELATING TO EQUITY.

UNITED STATES DISTRICT COURTS—JURISDICTION.

Suits in Equity to enforce Internal Revenue Taxes.
[Rev. Stat. 94.]

Sec. 563. The district court shall have jurisdiction as follows:

¶ 5. Of all suits in equity to enforce the lien of the United States upon any real estate for any internal revenue tax, or to subject to the payment of any such tax any real estate owned by the delinquent, or in which he has any right, title, or interest. (See sec. 3207.)

Suits to redress Deprivation of Rights.
[Rev. Stat. 95.]

¶ 12. Of all suits at law or in equity authorized by law to be brought by any person to redress the deprivation, under color of any law, ordinance, regulation, custom, or usage of any state, of any right, privilege, or immunity secured by the constitution of the United States, or of any right secured by any law of the United States to persons within the jurisdiction thereof. (See secs. 1977, 1979.)

Court always open for Certain Purposes.
[Rev. Stat. 101.]

Sec. 574. The district courts, as courts of admiralty, and as courts of equity, so far as equity jurisdiction has been conferred upon them, shall be deemed always open for the purpose of filing any pleading, or issuing and returning mesne and final process, and of making and directing all interlocutory motions, orders, rules, and other proceedings, preparatory to the hearing, upon their merits, of all causes pending therein. And any district judge may, upon reasonable notice to the parties, make, and direct and award, at chambers, or in the clerk's office, and in vacation as well as in term, all such process, commissions, orders, rules, and other proceedings, whenever the same are not grantable of course, according to the rules and practice of the court.

UNITED STATES CIRCUIT COURTS—JURISDICTION.

Aliens—Citizens of Different States.
[Rev. Stat. 109.]

Sec. 629. The circuit courts shall have jurisdiction as follows:

¶ 1. Of all suits of a civil nature at common law or in equity, where the matter in dispute, exclusive of costs, exceeds the sum or value of five hundred dollars, and an alien is a party, or the suit is between a citizen of the state where the suit is brought and a citizen of another state: *Provided*, that no circuit court shall have cognizance of any suit to recover the contents of any promissory note or other chose in action in favor of an assignee, unless a suit might have been prosecuted in such court to recover the said contents if no assignment had been made, except in cases of foreign bills of exchange.

Suits in Equity by the United States.
[Rev. Stat. 110.]

¶ 2. Of all suits in equity, where the matter in dispute, exclusive of costs, exceeds the sum or value of five hundred dollars, and the United States are petitioners.

Patent and Copyright Suits.

¶ 9. Of all suits at law or in equity arising under the patent or copyright laws of the United States.

Appeals.
[Rev. Stat. 112.]

Sec. 631. From all final decrees of a district court in causes of equity or of admiralty and maritime jurisdiction, except prize causes, where the matter in dispute exceeds the sum or value of fifty dollars, exclusive of costs, an appeal shall be allowed to the circuit court next to be held in such district, and such circuit court is required to receive, hear, and determine such appeal.

Copies of Proofs and Entries certified to Appellate Court.
[Rev. Stat. 112.]

Sec. 632. In case of an appeal, as provided by the preceding section, copies of the proofs, and of such entries and papers on file as may be necessary on hearing of the appeal, may be certified up to the appellate court.

Writs of Error and Appeals.
[Rev. Stat. 112.]

Sec. 635. No judgment, decree, or order of a district court shall be reviewed by a circuit court on writ of error or appeal, unless the writ of error is sued out, or the appeal is taken, within one year after the entry of such judgment, decree, or order: *Provided*, that when a party entitled to prosecute a writ of error or to take an appeal is an infant, or *non compos mentis*, or imprisoned, such writ of error may be prosecuted, or such appeal may be taken, within one year after the entry of the judgment, decree, or order, exclusive of the term of such disability. (See sec. 1008.)

Courts always open for Certain Purposes.
[Rev. Stat. 113.]

Sec. 638. The circuit courts, as courts of equity, shall be deemed always open for the purpose of filing any pleading, of issuing and returning mesne and final process, and of making and directing all interlocutory motions, orders, rules, and other proceedings, preparatory to the hearing, upon their merits, of all causes pending therein. And any judge of the circuit court may, upon reasonable notice to the parties, make, and direct and award, at chambers or in the clerk's office, and in vacation as well as in term, all such process, commissions, orders, rules, and other proceedings, whenever the same are not grantable of course, according to the rules and practice of the court.

Transcripts on Appeals.
[Rev. Stat. 130.]

Sec. 698. Upon the appeal of any cause in equity, or of admiralty and maritime jurisdiction, or of prize or no prize, a transcript of the record, as directed by law to be made, and copies of the proofs, and of such entries and papers on file as may be necessary on the hearing of the appeal, shall be transmitted to the Supreme Court: *Provided*, that either the court below or the Supreme Court may order any original document or other evidence to be sent up, in addition to the copy of the record, or, in lieu of a copy, of a part thereof. And on such appeals no new evidence shall be received in the Supreme Court, except in admiralty causes. (See sec. 750.)

When Suits in Equity may be maintained.
[Rev. Stat. 137.]

Sec. 723. Suits in equity shall not be sustained in either of the courts of the United States in any case where a plain, adequate, and complete remedy may be had at law.

Final Record—How made.
[Rev. Stat. 141.]

Sec. 750. In equity and admiralty causes, only the process, pleadings, and decree, and such orders and memorandums as may be necessary to show the jurisdiction of the court and regularity of the proceedings, shall be entered upon the final record. (See sec. 698.)

Mode of Proof.
[Rev. Stat. 162.]

Sec. 862. The mode of proof in causes of equity, and of admiralty and maritime jurisdiction, shall be according to rules now or hereafter prescribed by the Supreme Court, except as herein specially provided.

Mesne Process, and Proceedings in Equity.
[Rev. Stat. 173.]

Sec. 913. The forms of mesne process, and the forms and modes of proceeding in suits of equity, and of admiralty and maritime jurisdiction in the circuit and district courts, shall be according to the principles, rules, and usages which belong to courts of equity and of admiralty, respectively, except when it is otherwise provided by statute, or by rules of court made in pursuance thereof; but the same shall be subject to alteration and addition by the said courts, respectively, and to regulation by the Supreme Court, by rules prescribed, from time to time, to any circuit or district court, not inconsistent with the laws of the United States.

Power of the Supreme Court to regulate Practice.
[Rev. Stat. 174.]

Sec. 917. The Supreme Court shall have power to prescribe, from time to time, and in any manner not inconsistent with any law of the United States, the forms of writs and other process; the modes of framing and filing proceedings and pleadings; of taking and obtaining evidence; of obtaining discovery; of proceeding to obtain relief; of drawing up, entering, and enrolling decrees; and of proceeding before trustees appointed by the court, and generally to regulate the whole practice, to be used, in suits in equity or admiralty, by the circuit and district courts.

Writs of Error and Appeals to Supreme Court.
[Rev. Stat. 188.]

Sec. 1008. No judgment, decree, or order of a circuit or district court, in any civil action, at law or in equity, shall be reviewed in the Supreme Court on writ of error or appeal, unless the writ of error is brought, or the appeal taken within two years after the entry of such judgment, decree, or order: *Provided*, That where a party entitled to prosecute a writ of error, or to take an appeal, is an infant, insane person, or imprisoned, such writ of error may be prosecuted, or such appeal taken within two years after the judgment, decree, or order, exclusive of the term of such disability. (See sec. 635.)

CIVIL RIGHTS.

Equal Rights under the Law.
[Rev. Stat. 348.]

Sec. 1977. All persons within the jurisdiction of the United States shall have the same right in every state and territory to make and enforce contracts, to sue, be parties, give evidence, and to the full and equal benefit of all laws and proceedings for the security of persons and property, as is enjoyed by white citizens, and shall be subject to like punishment, pains, penalties, taxes, licenses, and exactions of every other kind, and to no other. (See sec. 563.)

Deprivation of Rights.

[Rev. Stat. 348.]

Sec. 1979. Every person who, under color of any statute, ordinance, regulation, custom, or usage of any state or territory, subjects, or causes to be subjected, any citizen of the United States, or other person within the jurisdiction thereof, to the deprivation of any rights, privileges, or immunities secured by the constitution and laws, shall be liable to the party injured, in an action at law, suit in equity, or other proper proceeding for redress. (See secs. 563, 629.)

INTERNAL REVENUE.

Proceedings to subject Payment of Tax.

[Rev. Stat. 619.]

Sec. 3207. In any case where there has been a refusal or neglect to pay any tax, and it has become necessary to seize and sell real estate to satisfy the same, the Commissioner of Internal Revenue may direct a bill in chancery to be filed, in a district or circuit court of the United States, to enforce the lien of the United States for tax upon any real estate, or to subject any real estate owned by the delinquent, or in which he has any right, title, or interest, to the payment of such tax. All persons having liens upon, or claiming any interest in the real estate sought to be subjected as aforesaid, shall be made parties to such proceedings, and be brought into court as provided in other suits in chancery therein. And the said court shall, at the term next after the parties have been duly notified of the proceedings, unless otherwise ordered by the court, proceed to adjudicate all matters involved therein, and finally determine the merits of all claims to, and liens upon the real estate in question, and, in all cases where a claim or interest of the United States therein is established, shall decree a sale of such real estate, by the proper officer of the court, and a distribution of the proceeds of such sale according to the findings of the court in respect to the interests of the parties and of the United States. (See sec. 563.)

FOREIGN RELATIONS.

Jurisdiction—How Exercised and Enforced.
[Rev. Stat. 793.]

Sec. 4086. Jurisdiction in both criminal and civil matters shall, in all cases, be exercised and enforced in conformity with the laws of the United States, which are hereby, so far as is necessary to execute such treaties, respectively, and so far as they are suitable to carry the same into effect, extended over all citizens of the United States in those countries, and over all others to the extent that the terms of the treaties, respectively, justify or require. But in all cases where such laws are not adapted to the object, or are deficient in the provisions necessary to furnish suitable remedies, the common law and the law of equity and admiralty shall be extended in like manner over such citizens and others in those countries; and if neither the common law, nor the law of equity or admiralty, nor the statutes of the United States, furnish appropriate and sufficient remedies, the ministers in those countries, respectively, shall, by decrees and regulations, which shall have the force of law, supply such defects and deficiencies.

PATENTS AND COPYRIGHTS.

Patents obtainable by Bill in Equity.
[Rev. Stat. 958.]

Sec. 4915. Whenever a patent on application is refused, either by the Commissioner of Patents or by the Supreme Court of the District of Columbia, upon appeal from the

Commissioner, the applicant may have remedy by bill in equity; and the court having cognizance thereof, on notice to adverse parties and other due proceedings had, may adjudge that such applicant is entitled, according to law, to receive a patent for his invention, as specified in his claim, or for any part thereof, as the facts in the case may appear. And such adjudication, if it be in favor of the right of the applicant, shall authorize the Commissioner to issue such patent on the applicant filing in the Patent Office a copy of the adjudication, and otherwise complying with the requirements of law. In all cases where there is no opposing party a copy of the bill shall be served on the Commissioner, and all the expenses of the proceeding shall be paid by the applicant, whether the final decision is in his favor or not. [See sec. 629.]

Suits touching Interfering Patents.

[Rev. Stat. 959.]

Sec. 4918. Whenever there are interferring patents, any person interested in any one of them, or in the working of the invention claimed under either of them, may have relief against the interfering patentee, and all parties interested under him, by suit in equity against the owners of the interfering patent; and the court, on notice to adverse parties and other due proceedings had, according to the course of equity, may adjudge and declare either of the patents void in whole or in part, or inoperative, or invalid, in any particular part of the United States, according to the interest of the parties in the patent or invention patented. But no such judgment or adjudication shall affect the right of any person except the parties to the suit and those deriving title under them subsequent to the rendition of such judgment.

Power of Courts to grant Injunctions and estimate Damages.

Rev. Stat. 960.]

Sec. 4921. The several courts vested with jurisdiction of cases arising under the patent laws shall have power to grant injunctions, according to the course and principles of courts of equity, to prevent the violation of any right secured by patent, on such terms as the court may deem reasonable; and upon a decree being rendered in any such case for an infringement, the complainant shall be entitled to recover, in addition to the profits to be accounted for by the defendant, the damages the complainant has sustained thereby; and the court shall assess the same or cause the same to be assessed under its direction. And the court shall have the same power to increase such damages, in its discretion, as is given to increase the damages found by verdicts in actions in the nature of actions of trespass upon the case.

Remedy for Infringement of Trade-marks.

[Rev. Stat. 964.]

Sec. 4942. Any person who shall reproduce, counterfeit, copy, or imitate any recorded trade-mark, and affix the same to goods of substantially the same descriptive properties and qualities as those referred to in the registration, shall be liable to an action on the case for damages for such wrongful use of such trade-mark, at the suit of the owner thereof; and the party aggrieved shall also have his remedy according to the course of equity to enjoin the wrongful use of his trade-mark and to recover compensation therefor, in any court having jurisdiction over the person guilty of such wrongful use.

BANKRUPTCY.

Power of District Courts to Compel Obedience.
[Rev. Stat. 970.]

Sec. 4975. The district courts of bankruptcy shall have full authority to compel obedience to all orders and decrees passed by them in bankruptcy, by process of contempt and other remedial process, to the same extent that the circuit courts now have in any suit pending therein in equity.

Appeals to Circuit Court.
[Rev. Stat. 970.]

Sec. 4980. Appeals may be taken from the district to the circuit courts in all cases in equity, and writs of error from the circuit courts to the district courts may be allowed in cases at law, arising under or authorized by this Title, when the debt or damages claimed amount to more than five hundred dollars; and any supposed creditor, whose claim is wholly or in part rejected, or an assignee who is dissatisfied with the allowance of a claim, may appeal from the decision of the district court to the circuit court for the same district.

Appeals—How taken.
[Rev. Stat. 970.]

Sec. 4981. No appeal shall be allowed in any case from the district to the circuit court unless it is claimed, and notice given thereof to the clerk of the district court, to be entered with the record of the proceedings, and also to the assignee or creditor, as the case may be, or to the defeated party in equity, within ten days after the entry of the decree or decision appealed from; nor unless the appellant at the time of claiming the same shall give bond in the manner required in cases of appeals in suits in equity; nor shall any writ of error be allowed unless the party claiming it shall comply with the provisions of law regulating the granting of such writs.

Appeal, how Entered.
[Rev. Stat. 971.]

Sec. 4982. Such appeal shall be entered at the term of the circuit court which shall be held within the district next after the expiration of ten days from the time of claiming the same.

Waiver of Appeal.
[Rev. Stat. 971.]

Sec. 4983. If the appellant, in writing, waives his appeal before any decision thereon, proceedings may be had in the district court as if no appeal had been taken.

Power of General Superintendence of Circuit Court.
[Rev. Stat. 971.]

Sec. 4986. The circuit court for each district shall have a general superintendence and jurisdiction of all cases and questions arising in the district court for such district when sitting as a court of bankruptcy, whether the powers and jurisdiction of a circuit court have been conferred on such district court or not; and, except when special provision is otherwise made, may, upon bill, petition, or other proper process, of any party aggrieved, hear and determine the case as in a court of equity; and the powers and jurisdiction hereby granted may be exercised either by the court in term time, or, in vacation, by the circuit justice or by the circuit judge of the circuit.

What Property vests in Assignee.
[Rev. Stat. 981.]

Sec. 5046. All property conveyed by the bankrupt in fraud of his creditors; all rights in equity, choses in action, patent-rights, and copy-rights; all debts due him, or any person for his use, and all liens and securities therefor; and all his rights of action for property or estate, real or personal, and for any cause of action which he had against any person arising from contract, or from the unlawful taking or detention, or injury to the property of the bankrupt, and all his rights of redeeming such property or estate, together with the like right, title, power, and authority to sell, manage, dispose of, sue for, and recover or defend the same, as the bankrupt might have had if no assignment had been made, shall, in virtue of the adjudication of bankruptcy, and the appointment of his assignee, but subject to the exceptions stated in the preceding section,[1] be at once vested in such assignee.

---

[1] Sec. 5045. There shall be excepted from the operation of the conveyance the necessary household and kitchen furniture, and such other articles and necessaries of the bankrupt as the assignee shall designate and set apart, having reference to the amount, to the family, condition, and circumstances of the bankrupt, but altogether not to exceed in value, in any case, the sum of five hundred dollars; also the wearing apparel of the bankrupt, and that of his wife and children, and the uniform, arms, and equipments of any person who is or has been a soldier in the militia, or in the service of the United States; and such other property as now is, or hereafter shall be, exempted from attachment, or seizure, or levy on execution, by the laws of the United States, and such other property, not included in the foregoing exceptions, as is exempted from levy and sale upon execution, or other process, or order of any court by the laws of the state in which the bankrupt has his domicile at the time of the commencement of the proceedings in bankruptcy, to an amount allowed by the constitution and laws of each state, as existing in the year eighteen hundred and seventy-one; and such exemptions shall be valid against debts contracted before the adoption and passage of such state constitution and laws, as well as those contracted after the same, and against liens by judgment or decree of any state court; any decision of any such court rendered since the adoption and passage of such constitution and laws to the contrary notwithstanding. These exceptions shall operate as a limitation upon the conveyance of the property of the bankrupt to his assignee; and in no case shall the property hereby excepted

Limitation to Suits in, by, and against Assignee.
[Rev. Stat. 982.]

Sec. 5057. No suit, either at law or in equity, shall be maintainable in any court between an assignee in bankruptcy and a person claiming an adverse interest, touching any property or rights of property transferable to or vested in such assignee, unless brought within two years from the time when the cause of action accrued for or against such assignee. And this provision shall not in any case revive a right of action barred at the time when an assignee was appointed.

---

pass to the assignee, or the title of the bankrupt thereto be impaired or affected by any of the provisions of this Title; and the determination of the assignee in the matter shall, on exception taken, be subject to the final decision of the said court.

ORDINANCES

MADE BY THE LORD CHANCELLOR BACON,

FOR THE BETTER AND MORE REGULAR ADMINISTRATION OF JUSTICE IN THE CHANCERY, TO BE DAILY OBSERVED, SAVING THE PREROGATIVE OF THE COURT.

1. No decree shall be reversed, altered or explained, being once under the great seal, but upon bill of review; and no bill of review shall be admitted, except it contain either error in law, appearing in the body of the decree, without further examination of matters in fact, or some new matter which hath risen in time after the decree, and not any new proof which might have been used when the decree was made: nevertheless, upon new proof, that is come to light after the decree made, and could not possibly have been used at the time when the decree passed, a bill of review may be grounded by the special license of the court, and not otherwise.

2. In case of miscasting, being a matter demonstrative, a decree may be explained, and reconciled by an order, without a bill of review; not understanding, by miscasting, any pretended misrating or misvaluing, but only error in the auditing or numbering.

3. No bill of review shall be admitted, or any other new bill, to change matter decreed, except the decree be first obeyed and performed: as, if it be for land, that the possession be yielded; if it be for money, that the money be paid: if it be for evidences, that the evidences be brought in; and so in other cases which stand upon the strength of the decree alone.

4. But if any act be decreed to be done which extinguisheth the parties' right at the common law, as making of assurance or release, acknowledging satisfaction, canceling of bonds or evidences, and the like; those parts of the decree are to be spared until the bill of review be determined; but such sparing is to be warranted by public order made in court.

5. No bill of review shall be put in, except the party that prefers it enter into recognizance with sureties for satisfying of costs and damages for the delay, if it be found against him.

6. No decrees shall be made, upon pretense of equity, against the express provision of an act of parliament: nevertheless, if the construction of such act of parliament hath for a time gone one way in general opinion and reputation, and after, by a later judgment, hath been controlled, then relief may be given upon matter of equity, for cases arising before the said judgment, because the subject was in no default.

7. Imprisonment for breach of a decree is in nature of an execution, and therefore the custody ought to be strait, and the party not to have any liberty to go abroad, but by special license of the lord chancellor; but no close imprisonment is to be, but by express order for willful and extraordinary contempts and disobedience, as hath been used.

8. In case of enormous and obstinate disobedience in breach of a decree, an injunction is to be granted "subpena" of a sum; and upon affidavit, or other sufficient proof, or persisting in contempt, fines are to be pronounced by the lord chancellor in open court, and the same to be estreated down into the hanaper, if cause be by a special order.

9. In case of a decree made for the possession of land, a writ of execution goes forth; and if that be disobeyed, then process of contempt according to the course of the

court against the person, unto a commission of rebellion; and then a sergeant-at-arms by special warrant: and in case the sergeant-at-arms can not find him, or be resisted; or upon the coming in of the party, and his commitment, if he persist in disobedience, an injunction is to be granted for the possession; and in case that also be disobeyed, then a commission to the sheriff to put him into possession.

10. Where a party is committed for the breach of a decree, he is not to be enlarged until the decree be fully performed in all things which are to be done presently. But if there be other parts of the decree to be performed at days, at times to come, then he may be enlarged by order of the court upon recognizance, with sureties to be put in for the performance thereof "*de futuro*," otherwise not.

11. Where causes come to a hearing in court, no decree bindeth any person who was not served with process "*ad audiendum judicium*," according to the course of the court, or did appear "*gratis*" in person in court.

12. No decree bindeth any that cometh in "*bona fide*," by conveyance from the defendant before the bill exhibited, and is made no party, neither by bill nor the order; but where he comes in "*pendente lite*," and while the suit is in full prosecution, and without any color of allowance or privity of the court, there regularly the decree bindeth; but if there were any intermission of suit, or the court made acquainted with the conveyance, the court is to give order upon the special matter according to justice.

13. Where causes are dismissed upon full hearing, and the dismission signed by the lord chancellor, such causes shall not be retained again, nor new bill exhibited, except it be upon new matter, like to the case of the bill of review.

14. In case of all other dismissions, which are not upon

hearing of the cause, if any new bill be brought, the dismission is to be pleaded, and after reference and report of the contents of both suits, and consideration taken of the former orders and dismission, the court shall rule the retaining and dismissing of the new bill, according to justice and nature of the case.

15. All suits grounded upon wills nuncupative, leases parol, or upon long leases that tend to the defeating of the king's tenures, or for the establishing of perpetuities, or grounded upon remainders put into the crown to defeat purchasers; or for brokage or rewards to make marriages; or for bargains at play and wagers; or for bargains for offices contrary to the statute of 5 and 6 Ed. VI., or for contracts upon usury or simony, are regularly to be dismissed upon motion, if they be the sole effect of the bill; and if there be no special circumstances to move the court to allow their proceedings, and all suits under the value of ten pounds are regularly to be dismissed. *V. postea*, secs. 58, 60.

16. Dismissions are properly to be prayed and had either upon hearing or upon plea unto the bill, when the cause comes first in court; but dismissions are not to be prayed after the parties have been at charge of examination, except it be upon special cause.

17. If the plaintiff discontinue the prosecution, after all the defendants have answered, above the space of one whole term, the cause is to be dismissed of course without any motion; but after replication put in, no cause is to be dismissed without motion and order of the court.

18. Double vexation is not to be admitted; but if the party sue for the same cause at the common law and in chancery, he is to have a day given to make his election where he will proceed, and in default of making such election to be dismissed.

19. Where causes are removed by special "*certiorari*" upon a bill containing matter of equity, the plaintiff is,

upon receipt of his writ, to put in bond to prove his suggestions within fourteen days after the receipt; which, if he do not prove, then upon certificate from either of the examiners, presented to the lord chancellor, the cause shall be dismissed with costs, and a "*procedendo*" to be granted.

20. No injunction of any nature shall be granted, revived, dissolved, or stayed upon any private petition.

21. No injunction to stay suits at the common law shall be granted upon priority of suit only, or upon surmise of the plaintiff's bill only; but upon matter confessed in the defendant's answer, or matter of record, or writing plainly appearing, or when the defendant is in contempt for not answering, or that the debt desired to be stayed appeareth to be old, and hath slept long, or the creditor or the debtor hath been dead some good time before the suit brought.

22. Where the defendant appears not, but sits an attachment; or when he doth appear and departs without answer, and is under attachment for not answering; or when he takes oath he can not answer without sight of evidences within the country; or where after answer he sues at common law by attorney, and absents himself beyond sea; in these cases an injunction is to be granted for the stay of all suits at the common law, until the party answer or appear in person in court, and the court give further order; but, nevertheless, upon answer put in, if there be no motion made the same term, or the next general seal after the term, to continue the injunction in regard of the insufficiency of the answer put in, or in regard of matter confessed in the answer, then the injunction to die and dissolve without any special order.

23. In the case aforesaid, where an injunction is to be awarded for stay of suits at the common law, if like suit be in the chancery, either by "*scire facias*," or privilege, or English bill, then the suit is to be stayed by order of

the court, as it is in other courts by injunction, for that the court can not enjoin itself.

24. Where an injunction hath been obtained for staying of suits, and no prosecution is had for the space of three terms, the injunction is to fall of itself without further motion.

25. Where a bill comes in after an arrest at the common law for debt, no injunction shall be granted without bringing the principal money into court, except there appear in the defendant's answer, or by sight of writings, plain matter tending to discharge the debt in equity; but if an injunction be awarded and disobeyed, in that case no money shall be brought in, or deposited, in regard of the contempt.

26. Injunctions for possession are not to be granted before a decree, but where the possession hath continued by the space of three years, before the bill exhibited, and upon the same title; and not upon any title, by lease, or otherwise determined.

27. In case where the defendant sits all the process of contempt, and can not be found by the sergeant-at-arms, or resists the sergeant, or makes rescue, a sequestration shall be granted of the land in question; and if the defendant render not himself within the year, then an injunction for the possession.

28. Injunctions against felling of timber, plowing up of ancient pastures, or for the maintaining of enclosures, or the like, shall be granted according to the circumstances of the case; but not in case where the defendant upon his answer claimeth an estate of inheritance, except it be where he claimeth the land in trust, or upon some other special ground.

29. No sequestration shall be granted but of lands, leases, or goods in question, and not of any other lands or goods not contained in the suits.

30. Where a decree is made for rent to be paid out of

land, or a sum of money to be levied out of the profits of land, there a sequestration of the same lands, being in the defendant's hands, may be granted.

31. Where the decrees of the provincial council, or of the court of requests, or the queen's court, are by contumacy or other means interrupted, there the court of chancery, upon a bill preferred for corroborations of the same jurisdictions, decrees and sentences, shall give remedy.

32. Where any cause comes to a hearing, that hath been formerly decreed in any other of the king's courts at Westminster, such decree shall be first read, and then to proceed to the rest of the evidence on both sides.

33. Suits after judgment may be admitted according to the ancient custom of the chancery, and the late royal decision of his majesty, of record, after solemn and great deliberation; but in such suits it is ordered, that bond be put in with good sureties to prove the suggestions of the bill.

34. Decrees upon suits brought after judgment shall contain no words to make void or weaken the judgment, but shall only correct the corrupt conscience of the party, and rule him to make restitution, or perform other acts, according to the equity of the cause.

35. The registers are to be sworn, as hath been lately ordered.

36. If any order shall be made, and the court not informed of the last material order formerly made, no benefit shall be taken by such order, as granted by abuse and surreption; and to that end the registers ought duly to mention the former order in the later.

37. No order shall be explained upon any private petition but in court as they are made, and the register is to set down the orders as they are pronounced by the court, truly, at his peril, without troubling the lord chancellor, by any private attending of him, to explain his meaning;

and if any explanation be desired, it is to be done by public motion, where the other party may be heard.

38. No draught of any order shall be delivered by the register to either party, without keeping a copy by him, to the end that if the order be not entered, nevertheless the court may be informed what was formerly done, and not put to new trouble and hearing; and to the end also that knowledge of orders be not kept back too long from either party, but may presently appear at the office.

39. Where a cause hath been debated upon hearing of both parties, and opinion hath been delivered by the court, and, nevertheless, the cause referred to treaty, the registers are not to admit the opinion of the court, in drawing of the order of reference, except the court doth especially declare that it be entered without any opinion either way; in which case, nevertheless, the registers are out of their short note to draw up some more full remembrance of that that passed in court, to inform the court if the cause come back and can not be agreed.

40. The registers, upon sending of their draught unto the counsel of the parties, are not to respect the interlineations or alterations of the said counsel, be the said counsel ever so great, farther than to put them in remembrance of that which was truly delivered in court, and so to conceive the order upon their oath and duty, without any further respect.

41. The registers are to be careful in the penning and drawing up of decrees, and special matters of difficulty and weight; and, therefore, when they present the same to the lord chancellor, they ought to give him understanding which are such decrees of weight, that they may be read and reviewed before his lordship sign them.

42. The decrees granted at the rolls are to be presented to his lordship, with the orders whereupon they are drawn, within two or three days after every term.

43. Injunctions for possession, or for stay of suits after

verdict, are to be presented to his lordship, together with the orders whereupon they go forth, that his lordship may take consideration of the order before he sign them.

44. Where any order upon the special nature of the case shall be made against any of these general rules, there the register shall plainly and expressly set down the particulars, reasons, and grounds moving the court to vary from the general use.

45. No reference upon demurrer or question touching the jurisdiction of the court shall be made to the masters of the chancery; but such demurrers shall be heard and ruled in court, or by the lord chancellor himself.

46. No order shall be made for the confirming or ratifying of any report without day first given, by the space of a seven-night at the least, to speak to it in court.

47. No reference shall be made to any masters of the court, or any other commissioners, to hear and determine, where the cause is gone so far as to examination of witnesses, except it be in special causes of parties near in blood, or of extreme poverty, or by consent and general reference of the estate of the cause, except it be by consent of the parties to be sparingly granted.

48. No report shall be respected in court which exceedeth the warrant of the order of reference.

49. The masters of the court are required not to certify the state of any cause, as if they would make breviate of the evidence on both sides, which doth little ease the court, but with some opinion; or, otherwise, in case they think it too doubtful to give opinion, and therefore make such special certificate, the cause is to go on to a judicial hearing without respect had to the same.

50. Matters of account, unless it be in very weighty causes, are not fit for the court, but to be prepared by reference, with this difference, nevertheless, that the

cause comes first to a hearing; and upon the entrance into a hearing, they may receive some direction, and be turned over to have the accounts considered, except both parties, before a hearing, do consent to a reference of the examination of the accounts, to make it more ready for a hearing.

51. The like course to be taken for the examination of court rolls upon customs and copies, which shall not be referred to any one master, but to two masters at the least.

52. No reference to be made of the insufficiency of an answer without showing of some particular point of the defect, and not upon surmise of the insufficiency in general.

53. Where a trust is confessed by the defendant's answer, there needeth no further hearing of the cause, but a reference presently to be made upon the account, and so to go on to hearing of the accounts.

54. In all suits where it shall appear, upon the hearing of the cause, that the plaintiff had not "*probabilem causam litigandi,*" he shall pay unto the defendant his utmost costs, to be assessed by the court.

55. If any bill, answer, replication, or rejoinder, shall be found of an immoderate length, both the party and the counsel under whose hand it passeth shall be fined.

56. If there be contained in any bill, answer, or other pleadings, or any interrogatory, any matter libellous or slanderous against any that is not a party to the suit, or against such as are parties to the suit, upon matters impertinent, or in derogation of the settled authorities of any of his majesty's court; such bills, answers, pleadings, or interrogatories, shall be taken off the file and suppressed, and the parties severally punished by commitment or ignominy, as shall be thought fit, for the abuse of the court; and the counselors at law, who have set

their hands, shall likewise receive reproof or punishment, if cause be.

57. Demurrers and pleas which tend to discharge the suit shall be heard first upon every day of orders, that the subject may know whether he shall need further attendance or no.

58. A demurrer is properly upon matter defective, contained in the bill itself, and no foreign matter; but a plea is of foreign matter to discharge or stay the suit, as that the cause hath been formerly dismissed, or that the plaintiff is outlawed, or excommunicated; or there is another bill depending for the same cause, or the like; and such plea may be put in without oath, in case where the matter of the plea appear upon record; but if it be anything that doth not appear upon record, the plea must be upon oath.

59. No plea of outlawry shall be allowed without pleading the record "*sub pede sigilli;*" nor plea of excommunication, without the seal of the ordinary.

60. Where any suit appeareth upon the bill to be of the natures which are regularly to be dismissed according to the fifteenth ordinance, such matter is to be set forth by way of demurrer.

61. Where an answer shall be certified insufficient, the defendant is to pay costs; and if a second answer be returned insufficient, in the points before certified insufficient, then double costs, and upon the third, treble costs, and upon the fourth, quadruple costs, and then to be committed also until he hath made a perfect answer, and to be examined upon interrogatories touching the points defective in his answer; but if any answer be certified sufficient, the plaintiff is to pay costs.

62. No insufficient answer can be taken hold of after replication put in, because it is admitted sufficient by the replication.

63. An answer to a matter charged as the defendant's

own fact must be direct, without saying it is to his remembrance, or as he believeth, if it be laid down within seven years before; and if the defendant deny the fact, he must traverse it directly, and not by way of negative pregnant; as if a fact be laid to be done with divers circumstances, the defendant may not traverse it literally as it is laid in the bill, but must traverse the point of substance; so if he be charged with the receipt of one hundred pounds, he must traverse that he hath not received a hundred pounds, or any part thereof; and if he have received part, he must set forth what part.

64. If a hearing be prayed upon bill and answer, the answer must be admitted to be true in all points, and a decree ought not to be made, but upon hearing the answer read in court.

65. Where no counsel appears for the defendant at the hearing, and the process appears to have been served, the answer of such defendant is to be read in court.

66. No new matter is to be contained in any replication, except it be to avoid matter set forth in the defendant's answer.

67. All copies in chancery shall contain fifteen lines in every sheet thereof, written orderly and unwastefully, unto which shall be subscribed the name of the principal clerk of the office where it is written, or his deputy, for whom he will answer, for which only subscription no fee at all shall be taken.

68. All commissions for examination of witnesses shall be "*super interr. inclusis*" only, and no return of depositions into the court shall be received but such only as shall be either compromised in one roll, subscribed with the name of the commissioners, or else in divers rolls, whereof each one shall be so subscribed.

69. If both parties join in commission, and upon warning given the defendant bring his commissioners, but produceth no witnesses, nor ministereth interroga-

tories, but after seek a new commission, the same shall not be granted; but, nevertheless, upon some extraordinary excuse of the defendant's default, he may have liberty granted by special order to examine his witnesses in court upon the former interrogatories, giving the plaintiff or his attorney notice that he may examine also if he will.

70. The defendant is not to be examined upon interrogatories, except it be in very special cases, by express order of the court, to sift out some fraud or practice pregnantly appearing to the court, or otherwise upon offer of the plaintiff to be concluded by the answer of the defendant without any liberty to disprove such answer, or to impeach him after a perjury.

71. Decrees in other courts may be read upon hearing without the warrant of any special order; but no depositions taken in any other court are to be read but by special order; and regularly the court granteth no order for reading of depositions, except it be between the same parties, and upon the same title and cause of suit.

72. No examination is to be had of the credit of any witness but by special order, which is sparingly to be granted.

73. Witnesses shall not be examined "*in perpetuam rei memoriam,*" except it be on the ground of a bill first put in, an answer thereunto made, and the defendant or his attorney made acquainted with the names of the witnesses that the plaintiff would have examined, and so publication to be of such witnesses; and this restraint nevertheless, that no benefit shall be taken of the depositions of such witnesses, in case they may be brought "*viva voce*" upon the trial, but only to be used in case of death before the trial, or age, or impotency, or absence out of the realm at the trial.

74. No witnesses shall be examined after publication, except it be by consent or by special order, "*ad informan-*

dam conscientiam judiciis," and then to be brought, close sealed, up to the court to peruse or publish, as the court shall think good.

75. No affidavit shall be taken or admitted by any master of the chancery tending to the proof or disproof of the title or matter in question, or touching the merits of the cause; neither shall any such matter be colorably inserted in any affidavit for serving of process.

76. No affidavit shall be taken against affidavit, as far as the masters of chancery can have knowledge; and if any such be taken, the latter affidavit shall not be used nor read in court.

77. In case of contempt grounded upon force or ill words upon serving of process, or upon words of scandal of the court proved by affidavit, the party is forthwith to stand committed; but, for other contempts against the orders or decrees of the court, an attachment goes forth: first, upon an affidavit made, and then the party is to be examined upon interrogatories, and his examination referred; and if, upon his examination, he confess matter of contempt, he is to be committed; if not, the adverse party may examine witnesses to prove the contempt; and, therefore if the contempt appear, the party is to be committed; but, if not, or if the party that pursues the contempt do fail in putting in interrogatories, or other prosecution, or fail in the proof of the contempt, then the party charged with the contempt is to be discharged with good costs.

78. They that are in contempt, specially so far as proclamation of rebellion, are not to be heard, neither in that suit, nor any other, except the court of special grace suspend the contempt.

79. Imprisonment upon contempt for matters past, may be discharged of grace after sufficient punishment or otherwise dispensed with; but, if the imprisonment be for not performance of any order of the court in force,

they ought not to be discharged except they first obey, but the contempt may be suspended for a time.

80. Injunctions, sequestration, dismissions, retainers upon dismissions, or final orders, are not to be granted upon petitions.

81. No former order made in court is to be altered, crossed, or explained upon any petition; but such orders may be stayed upon petition for a small stay, until the matter may be moved in court.

82. No commission for examination of witnesses shall be discharged, nor no examinations or depositions shall be suppressed upon petition, except it be upon point of course of the court first referred to the clerks, and certificate thereupon.

83. No demurrer shall be overruled upon petition.

84. No "*scire facias*" shall be awarded upon recognizances not enrolled, nor upon recognizances enrolled, unless it be upon examination of the record with the writ; nor no recognizance shall be enrolled after the year, except it be upon special order from the lord chancellor.

85. No writ of "*ne exeat regnum*," prohibition, consultation, statute of Northampton, "*certiorari*" special, "*procedendo*" special, or "*certiorari*" or "*procedendo*" general, more than once in the same cause; "habeas corpus," or "*corpus cum causa, vi laica removenda*," or restitution thereupon, "*de coronatore et viridario eligendo*," in case of a moving "*de homine repleg. assiz.*" or special patent, "*de ballivo amovena', certiorari ouper præsentationibus fact. coram commissariis sewar'*," or "*ad quod dampnum*," shall pass without warrant under the lord chancellor's hand, and signed by him, save such writs "*ad quod dampnum*," as shall be signed by Master Attorney.

86. Writs of privilege are to be reduced to a better rule, both for the number of persons that shall be privileged, and for the case of the privilege; and as for the number, it shall be set down by schedule; for the case, it

is to be understood, that besides persons privileged as attendants upon the court, suitors and witnesses are only to have privilege "*eundo, redeundo, et morando*," for their necessary attendance, and not otherwise; and that such writ of privilege dischargeth only an arrest upon the first process, but yet, where at such times of necessary attendance the party is taken in execution, it is a contempt to the court, and accordingly to be punished.

87. No "*supplicavit*" for the good behavior shall be granted, but upon articles grounded upon the oath of two at the least, or certificate upon any one justice of assize, or two justices of the peace, with affidavit that it is their hands, or by order of the Star Chamber, or chancery, or other of the king's courts.

88. No recognizance of the good behavior, or the peace, taken in the country, and certified into the petty-bag, shall be filed in the year without warrant from the lord chancellor.

89. Writs of "*ne exeat regnum*" are properly to be granted according to the suggestion of the writ, in respect of attempts prejudicial to the king and state, in which case the lord chancellor will grant them upon prayer of any of the principal secretaries without cause showing, or upon such information as his lordship shall think of weight; but otherwise also they may be granted, according to the practice of long time used, in case of interlopers in trade, great bankrupts, in whose estate many subjects are interested, or other cases that concern multitudes of the king's subjects, also in cases of duels, and divers others.

90. All writs, certificates, and whatsoever other process "*ret. coram Rege in Canc.*" shall be brought into the chapel of the rolls, within convenient time after the return thereof, and shall be there filed upon their proper files and bundles as they ought to be; except the depositions of witnesses, which may remain with any of the

six clerks by the space of one year next after the cause shall be determined by decree, or otherwise be dismissed.

91. All injunctions shall be enrolled, or the transcript filed, to the end that, if occasion be, the court may take order to award writs of "*scire facias*" thereupon, as in ancient time hath been used.

92. All days given by the court to sheriffs to return their writs, or bring in their prisoners upon writs of privilege, or otherwise between party and party, shall be filed, either in the register's office, or in the petty-bag respectively; and all recognizances, taken to the king's use or unto the court, shall be duly enrolled in convenient time with the clerks of the enrollment, and calendars made of them, and the calendars every Michaelmas term to be presented to the lord chancellor.

93. In case of suits upon the commission for charitable uses, to avoid charge, there shall need no bill, but only exceptions to the decree, an answer forthwith to be made thereunto; and thereupon, and upon sight of the inquisition, and the decree brought unto the lord chancellor by the clerk of the petty-bag, his lordship, upon perusal thereof, will give order under his hand for an absolute decree to be drawn up.

94. Upon suit for the commission of sewers, the names of those that are desired to be commissioners are to be presented to the lord chancellor in writing; then his lordship will send the name of some privy counselor, lieutenant of the shire, or justices of assize, being resident in the parts for which the commission is prayed, to consider of them, that they be not put in for private respects; and upon the return of such opinion, his lordship will give further order for the commission to pass.

95. No new commission of sewers shall be granted while the first is in force, except it be upon discovery of abuse or fault in the first commissioners, or otherwise upon some great or weighty ground.

96. No commission of bankrupt shall be granted but upon petition first exhibited to the lord chancellor, together with names presented, of which his lordship will take consideration, and always mingle some learned in the law with the rest; yet so as care be taken that the same parties be not too often used in commissions; and likewise care is to be taken that bond with good security be entered into, in £200 at least, to prove him a bankrupt.

97. No commission of delegates in any cause of weight shall be awarded, but upon petition preferred to the lord chancellor, who will name the commissioners himself, to the end they may be persons of convenient quality, having regard to the weight of the cause and the dignity of the court from whence the appeal is.

98. Any man shall be admitted to defend "*in forma pauperis,*" upon oath, but for plaintiffs they are ordinarily to be referred to the courts of request, or to the provincial councils, if the case arise in those jurisdictions, or to some gentlemen in the country, except it be in some special cases of commiseration, or potency of the adverse party.

99. Licenses to collect for losses by fire or water are not to be granted, but upon good certificate; and not for decays, or suretyship, or debt, or any other casualties whatsoever, and they are rarely to be renewed; and they are to be directed ever unto the county where the loss did arise, if it were by fire, and the counties that abut upon it, as the case shall require; and if it were by sea, then unto the county where the port is from whence the ship went, and to some sea-counties adjoining.

100. No exemplification shall be made of letters patent, "*inter alia,*" with omission of the general words; nor of records made void or canceled; nor of the decrees of this court not enrolled; nor of depositions by parcel and fractions, omitting the residue of the depositions in court, to which the hand of the examiner is not subscribed; nor

the records of the court not being enrolled or filed; nor of records of any other court, before the same be duly certified to this court, and orderly filed here; nor of any records upon the sight and examination of any copy in paper, but upon sight and examination of the original.

101. And because time and experience may discover some of these rules to be inconvenient, and some other to be fit to be added; therefore his lordship intendeth in any such case from time to time to publish any such revocations or additions.

INDEX.

ABATEMENT—
  When abatement of a suit takes place, and how revived, ... 134
  Where the interest transmitted may be contested, 136

ACCOUNT—
  Why matters of account cognizable in equity, [note] 37
    "   " 37

ACCIDENT—
  When cognizable in equity, ... 37

AFFIDAVIT—
  When necessary to be annexed to a bill, . . 51
    "   "   "   "   "   . . 70
    "   "   "   "   "   . . 77
  Form of, ... 64

AGREEMENTS—
  Equity may decree the specific performance of, 36

AMENDMENTS—
  Liberality of courts of equity in allowing, 124
  When necessary, ... 124
  When bill may be amended as of course, . 125
  What must be stated in an amended bill, . . 125
  Rule as to permitting amendments of answers, . 125

ANSWER—
  In what cases necessary, ... 111
  Nature of an answer, ... 111
  Parts of an answer, ... 111
  Defendant must answer fully, if at all, . . 111
  Matters which a defendant can not be required to answer, ... 111

Form of an answer,	112
Titles of answers,	113
Commencements of answer,	114
Conclusions of answer,	114
When answer must be sworn to by defendant,	115
How answer of a corporation is put in,	115
How an infant answers,	115
May put in a new answer when he becomes of age,	115
How a married woman answers,	115
Amendment of answer, see AMENDMENT.	
When answer not necessary to a bill of review,	172
Answer of the respondent in an appeal,	176
Insufficiency of answer, see EXCEPTIONS TO ANSWER.	
Mode of taking answer, see COMMISSION; EXAMINER.	

APPEAL—

To what tribunal appeals from the chancellor allowed,	174
When allowed for the first time,	174
No writ necessary in cases of,	175
Foundation of this rule,	175
Right of appeal in England depends upon enrollment of decree, [note]	175
Extends to interlocutory as well as final decrees,	175
In United States only extends to final decrees,	175
An appeal does not of itself suspend proceedings in England,	175
Rule otherwise, generally, in America,	175
Form of a petition for appeal,	175
Form of respondent's answer,	176
Course of proceedings on,	177
No new evidence can be admitted on,	177
Effect of decree upon hearing of,	177

APPEARANCE—

Definition of,	85
Ancient form of, [note]	85
Mode of compelling an appearance,	86
When appearance may be dispensed with,	86
Case illustrating the chain of process to compel an appearance, [note]	93

ARTICLES—
Form of articles of exception to the credit of a witness, ... 146

ATTACHMENT—
Nature and use of the process of attachment, 87
Form of an attachment, . . . 87
How it differs from a capias at common law. . [note] 87
To what it answers in the civil law, . . 87
Is not executed upon the persons of peers or infants, ... [note] 88
The return of an attachment, . . . 88

ATTACHMENT WITH PROCLAMATIONS—
When required, ... 88
Form of, ... 89

ATTORNEYS—
Historical account of the ancient mode of appearance by, ... [note] 85

BAILMENTS—
In cases of, bill of interpleader does not lie in equity, ... [note] 70

BILL IN EQUITY—
Nature of, ... 40
Answers to a declaration at common law, or libel at the civil law, ... 40
How it differs from an information, . . 40
Form of an ancient bill, . . . [note] 40
Historical accounts of ancient bills, . [note] 41
By whom it may be filed, ... 42
In case of infant or married woman, it may be filed by next friend, ... 42
In case of idiot or lunatic by committee, . 42

BILLS OF EQUITY, DIVISION OF—
Distinction between original bills and bills not original, 42
Original bills divided into such as pray relief and such as do not, ... 42
Form of a bill in equity, by what determined, . 43
Is constituted of nine distinct parts, . . 43
To whom it should be addressed, . . . 43

INDEX.

Form of address, ... 51
What should be contained in the introduction, . 43
Form of, ... 51
Description of the parties, ... 43
Object of this, ... 43
Averment where suit is in the federal courts, . 43
What should be contained in the premises, . . 44
Form of, ... 51
Narrative of the complainant, . . 44
Deeds should not be set forth *in hæc verba*, . . 44
Circumstances which must be averred with certainty, 44
What is contained in the charge of confederacy, . 44
Form of, ... 52
Insertion of this charge unnecessary, . . . 44
Origin of the practice, ... 44
What is contained in the charging part, . 45
Form of, ... 53
Use of this part of the bill, ... 45
Origin and recent introduction of, . . 45
Rule of the Supreme Court as to insertion of, 45
What is contained in the averment of jurisdiction, 45
Form of, ... 53
Object of this averment, ... 45
It is in all cases unnecessary, . . . 46
What is contained in the interrogating part, . 46, 47
Form of, ... 54
What must be answered under general interrogatories, 46
Use of specific interrogatories, . . . 46
Provision of Supreme Court in reference to, . 47
What must be contained in the prayer for relief, 47
Form of, ... 55
Difference between the prayer for general and special
  relief, ... 47
What is embraced by prayer for general relief, 47
When prayer for specific relief necessary, . 47
Safest practice is to include both, . . . 48
What is contained in the prayer of process, . 48, 49
Form of, ... 56
Rules of Supreme Court in reference to, . . 48

Persons not considered parties to a suit in England unless process is paid against them,	48
Of parties to a bill in equity, see PARTIES.	
Bill must be signed by counsel,	50
Bills formerly perused by court before they were filed,	50
Scandalous or irrelevant matter expunged,	51
When a bill must be accompanied by affidavit,	51
See AFFIDAVIT.	
Form of an original bill,	51
Form of an original bill framed according to the rules of the Supreme Court,	56
Commencement of bills,	59
Prayers of bills,	60, 64
Form of bill to foreclose a mortgage,	65
General observations on, [*note*]	65
Form of a bill for specific performance,	66
Form of a bill for a settlement and receiver between partners,	68
See INTERPLEADER; CERTIORARI; TESTIMONY; DISCOVERY; SUPPLEMENTAL BILL; REVIVOR; REVIEW; CROSS-BILL.	
Bill to impeach a decree of fraud,	172
When proper,	172
Frame of,	172
Bills to carry a decree into execution,	173
When necessary,	173

BAR. See PLEAS.

CAVEAT—

Object of, to prevent the enrollment of a decree,	163

CERTIORARI, BILL OF—

Object of,	73
Statements and frame of,	73
Prays no subpœna, and why,	73
Proceedings on,	74
Conclusion of,	74
Form of the writ of certiorari,	74

CHANCELLOR—

Historical sketch of his office. [*notes*]	27 and 31

CHANCERY—
Rise and progress of its equitable jurisdiction, . 25
Sketch of the same by Sir James Macintosh, [*note*] 31
Historical notice of the Chancellors, . . . 30
Matters cognizable in the court, . . 32 to 39
Distribution of its jurisdiction between various courts in England and the United States, . . [*note*] 38

CIVIL LAW—
Origin of its introduction into Courts of Equity, . 37

COMMISSION OF REBELLION—
When necessary, ... 89
Reason of its being directed to commissioners, [*note*] 89

COMMISSION TO TAKE ANSWER—
Form of, ... 118

COMMISSION TO EXAMINE WITNESSES—
When necessary, ... 139
Form of, ... 140

CONTEMPT—
Description of the several processes of, . . 86

CORPORATION—
Prayer of process against, ... 48
Mode of compelling appearance, . . 94

COUNSEL—
Required to sign bill, . . . 50

CROSS BILL—
When necessary for the purpose of defense, . . 115
May be exhibited for relief as well as discovery, 115
When it is necessary to allege any ground of equitable jurisdiction, ... 116
To what analogous in the canon law, . . 116
Form of, ... 116

DECREE—
When rendered *pro confesso*, . . . 86
Form of a decree *pro confesso*, . . [*note*] 156
Proper course in rendering such decree, . . 154
Difference between a final and interlocutory decree 152, 174

Definition of a decree, ... 152
Decrees which, though final in their nature, require
    further action, ... 154
Nature of a decree *nisi*, ... 154
Method of taking and recording decree, . [*note*] 154
Formal parts of a decree, ... 155
Form of a decree by default, ... 157
Form of a decree for an account, . . . 157
Form of a decree for a specific performance, . . 158
Form of a decree in a creditor's suit, . . 159
Form of a decree of interpleader, . . . 159
Decree of sale on foreclosure of a mortgage, . 160
Mode of enrolling a decree, and time within which it
    may be done, ... 162
Practice in the United States . . . [*note*] 162
Form of a decree upon a re-hearing, . . . 164

DEDIMUS POTESTATEM—See COMMISSION TO TAKE ANSWER.

DEFENSE—
  Various kinds of, to a suit in equity, ... 98
  Modern doctrine as to the extent to which they may
    be united in the same bill, ... 98
  Must be signed by counsel, ... 106

DEMURRER—
  When it is a proper mode of defense, . . . 100
  Nature and use of, ... 100
  Effect of the allowance of a demurrer to the whole
    bill, ... 100
  What should be stated in a demurrer, . . . 100
  Any number of causes may be assigned for a demurrer, ... 101
  Demurrer may be either to the relief or the discovery,
    or both, ... 101
  Rule in England when a party entitled to discovery
    asks for relief also, ... 101
  American rule, ... 101
  Grounds of demurrer to bills for relief, . . . 101

1. That the case in the bill is not one fit for equitable cognizance,	101
2. That the plaintiff is under a disability to sue,	102
3. That the plaintiff has no interest in the suit,	102
4. The want of privity between the parties,	102
5. That the defendant has no interest in the subject,	102
6. The want of necessary parties,	102
7. The multifariousness of the bill,	102
Grounds of demurrer to bills for discovery,	103
1. That the case is not one in which equity will compel a discovery,	103
2. That the plaintiff has no interest on which to found a right to a discovery,	103
3. That the defendant may be a witness,	103
4. That the discovery would be immaterial,	103
Form of a general demurrer,	103
Origin of the protestation clause in demurrers, [*note*]	103
Form of a demurrer for want of privity,	104
" " " for multifariousness,	104
" " " for want of parties,	105
Demurerr to a bill of discovery,	105
Demurrer coupled with answer,	106
Demurrer is not sworn to,	106
But can not be filed in courts of United States, save on certificate of counsel,	106
When usual mode of answer to bills of review,	172

DEPOSITIONS—

When taken by examiner, and when taken by commissioners,	139

SEE COMMISSION.

Form of interrogatories,	141
Form in which depositions are taken by commission,	143
Form in which taken before an examiner,	144
Manner in which depositions are returned,	147
What is meant by passing publication of depositions,	145

DISCLAIMER—

Definition of,	98
Will protect a mere witness from answering,	98

INDEX. 259

But can not avoid a liability,	98
Form of simple disclaimer,	98
Can scarcely ever be put in without answer, [*note*]	99
Form of an answer in connection with, [*note*]	99

DISTRINGAS—
For what purpose used in equity,	94
Form of,	95

DISCOVERY, BILL OF—
What is emphatically so called,	76
Is in general ancillary to another jurisdiction,	76
What should be stated in a bill of discovery,	76
When it is necessary to aver that a discovery is essential to maintain a suit at law,	76
Cases in which an affidavit must accompany the bill,	76
Form of a bill of discovery,	77

DOWER—
Why assignable in equity, [*note*]	36

EXAMINATION OF WITNESSES—
And examiner,	139

See COMMISSION; DEPOSITIONS.

ENROLLMENT OF DECREE. See DECREE.

EXCEPTION TO ANSWER—
In what cases they may be preferred,	120
This proceeding peculiar to courts of equity,	120
How drawn and what stated in,	121
Can not be taken to answer of infant,	121
When answer is open to exception,	121
Form of exceptions to answer,	121
Within what time to be filed,	122
How validity of exceptions to be determined,	122
Deference to a master,	122
Form of exceptions to his report,	122
Exceptions to credit of witnesses,	146

EXECUTION OF DECREES—
Bill to carry decree into execution,	173
Ancient mode of enforcing decrees, [*note*]	166
General principle in reference to,	166
Mode where decree is *in personam*,	166

Where decree is *in rem*,	167
Form of a writ of execution,	167
Form of a writ of injunction to deliver land,	168

FRAUD—
When cognizable in equity,	37

HEARING OF A CAUSE—
Cause may be set down for hearing by either party,	148
Use of subpœna to hear judgment,	148
Form of,	148
When returnable, and meaning of "days of grace,"	149
Course of proceeding at the hearing,	149
Where the defendant fails to attend,	150
Where the plaintiff fails to attend, [*note*]	150

INFORMATION—
How it differs from a bill,	78
Its form,	78
When the name of the relator is inserted,	79

INJUNCTION—
Must be especially asked for in bill, when required,	48
Prayer for,	60
Form of a writ, [*note*]	60
Injunction for performance of decree,	168

INTERROGATORIES FOR EXAMINATION OF WITNESSES—
How to be framed,	141
Form of,	141

INTERLOCUTORY BILLS—
Are such as arise between the institution and final determination of a suit,	133

See SUPPLEMENTAL BILL; REVIVOR, BILL OF.

INTERLOCUTORY PROCEEDINGS—
Nature of,	124
May be made by motion or petition,	124
Address to the discretion of the court,	124
When to be supported by affidavit,	124

See AMENDMENT; RECEIVER; REFERENCE TO A MASTER; PAYMENT OF MONEY INTO COURT.

INTERPLEADER, BILL OF—

In what case and for what purpose exhibited,	70
Affidavit must accompany the bill denying collusion,	70
An offer must be made to bring money due into court,	71
What must be shown by the bill,	71
Plaintiff only entitled to a decree that the bill was properly filed,	71
Subsequent course of proceeding,	71
Form of a bill of interpleader,	71

ISSUE—

What it is, and whence borrowed,	152
How framed,	153
Proceedings on,	153

JURISDICTION OF EQUITY—

General description of,	34
Lord Redesdale's classification, [note]	35
How a question of jurisdiction can be determined,	38

KING—

Originally presided in the *Aula Regis*,	26

LABEL—

What it is,	82
Upon whom it may be served,	82

LETTER MISSIVE—

Origin of the practice of sending, [note]	83
To whom it is sent,	82
Form of,	83
Is not considered a process,	83

MESSENGER—

When one is employed in equity,	88

NE EXEAT REGNO—

Form of prayer for one,	63
Form of the writ,	63
Must be specially asked for in bill,	48

ORDERS—

Form of, for production of papers,	127
Form of, that plaintiff elect,	127
Form of, to pay money into court,	127
Form of order of reference to master,	128

PARTIES—

Those only are considered such in England against whom process is prayed,	48
Rule in New York,	48
General rule as to who must be,	49
Grounds of exception to this rule,	49
1. Where bill seeks a discovery of them,	49
2. Where party is out of the jurisdiction,	49
3. Where the parties are very numerous,	49
Subdivision of this class of cases,	49
Consequence of a failure to make the proper parties,	50
Mode of making the objection,	50

PAYMENT OF MONEY INTO COURT—

Cases in which this order will be made,	126
Disposition of such fund by the court,	126

PETITION—

For rehearing a cause in equity,	164
What must be stated in it,	163

PLEAS—

Definition, object, and form of,	106
Several kinds of,	107
1. To the jurisdiction, nature of,	107
What must be shown in,	108
2. To the person, averments of,	108
3. To the frame of the bill,	108
4. Pleas in bar,	108
Bar by statute, by record, or by matter *in pais*,	107
The pendency of a suit at law not a good plea to the bill, [*note*]	108
Form of,	109
Pendency of another bill,	110
Plea of infancy to bill exhibited without *prochein ami*,	110
Plea of coverture of plaintiff,	110
Mode of objecting to,	110
Amendment of,	111

PRAYERS OF BILLS—

General observations upon,	47

Form to restrain proceedings at law, and for an injunction, ... 60
For an account of the rents and profits of real estate, 61
For an account of money had and received, . . 62
For the production of deeds and papers, . . 62
For an account of personal estate, . . . 62
For the writ of *ne exeat*, ... 63
Form of prayers in suit against a State or the United States, ... 64
Form in suits against a corporation, . . . 64

PROCESS—
General observations upon the prayer for, . . 48
Chain of process illustrated, . . . [*note*] 93

RECEIVER—
Cases in which the court will appoint one, . . 125
It must appear by affidavit that the fund or property is in danger, ... 125

REFERENCE TO A MASTER—
Cases in which this is usual, ... 126
Advantages of it to a chancellor, . . 126
Powers of the master under the commission, . . 126

REHEARING—
Manner in which it is obtained in equity, . . 163
Proceedings upon the rehearing, . . . 164
See PETITION.

REJOINDER—
Nature of, ... 131
Not in general necessary, ... 131
Form of, ... 131

REPLICATION—
Difference between a general and special replication, 129
Form of a general replication, ... 130
Form of a special replication, ... 130
Proceedings after replication, ... 131

REPORT OF A MASTER—
Mode of taking exceptions to, ... 122

RETURN—
  Return day of a subpena to appear, . . *[note] 81
  Return day of a subpena to hear judgment, . . 149
REVIEW—
  Bill of, when proper, ... 170
  Form of the bill of review, ... [note] 171
  Period within which it may be brought, . . 170
  What must be recited in, ... 171
  Proceedings upon, ... 170
REVIVOR—
  Bill of, when necessary, ... 134
  Familiar cases of, ... 134
  Form of, ... 135
  How it differs from a bill in the nature of a bill of revivor, ... 136
  Form of statement in latter bill, ... 137
SEQUESTRATION—
  In what cases awarded in equity, . . . 91
  History of its introduction, . . . [note] 91
  Form of, ... 92
  Manner in which it is served, ... 92
  Consequence of awarding a sequestration against a corporation, ... 95
  Used to compel performance of a decree, . . 167
SERGEANT-AT-ARMS—
  Duties of this officer, ... 91
SERVICE. See SUBPENA.
SUBPENA—
  Origin of, and history of its introduction, . 80
  Form of, to appear and answer, ... 80
  Number of defendants introduced in, . [note] 81
  Return day of, ... [note] 81
  Mode of serving the subpena, ... 84
  Discussion of the question whether subpena may be served in a foreign country, . . [note] 84
  Subpena to hear judgment, form of, . . . 148
  Form of subpena to show cause, ... 150
  Subpena to rejoin, object of, ... 131

SUPPLEMENTAL BILL—
   When, and for what purpose used, . 133
   Form of, so far as it is peculiar, ... 135
   Difference between, and an original bill in the nature
      of a supplemental bill, ... 137
   Statement in the latter bill, ... 137
   Difference between it and an original bill in the nature
      of a bill of revivor, ... 137

TESTIMONY, BILL TO PERPETUATE—
   When it is necessary, ... 75
   Conformable to the usage of the Roman law, 75
   Form and averments of, ... 75

WITNESSES—
   Exceptions to credit of, how taken, . [*note*] 146

www.ingramcontent.com/pod-product-compliance
Lightning Source LLC
Chambersburg PA
CBHW032134230426
43672CB00011B/2337